DANGLING IN THE GLIMMER OF HOPE

DANGLING IN THE GLIMMER OF HOPE

Academic Action on Truth and Reconciliation

Edited by Garry Gottfriedson
and Victoria Handford

University of Ottawa Press
2024

Les Presses de l'Université d'Ottawa
University of Ottawa Press

The University of Ottawa Press (UOP) is proud to be the oldest of the francophone university presses in Canada and the oldest bilingual university publisher in North America. Since 1936, UOP has been enriching intellectual and cultural discourse by producing peer-reviewed and award-winning books in the humanities and social sciences, in French and in English.

www.Press.uOttawa.ca

Library and Archives Canada Cataloguing in Publication

Title: Dangling in the glimmer of hope : academic action on Truth and Reconciliation / edited by Garry Gottfriedson and Victoria Handford.
Names: Gottfriedson, Garry, 1954- editor. | Handford, Victoria, 1957- editor.
Description: Includes bibliographical references.
Identifiers: Canadiana (print) 20240303245 | Canadiana (ebook) 20240304098 | ISBN 9780776644653 (hardcover) | ISBN 9780776644660 (softcover) | ISBN 9780776644684 (EPUB) | ISBN 9780776644677 (PDF)
Subjects: LCSH: Critical pedagogy—Canada. | LCSH: Transformative learning—Canada. | LCSH: Culturally relevant pedagogy—Canada. | LCSH: Culturally sustaining pedagogy—Canada. | LCSH: Indigenous peoples—Education—Canada. | LCSH: Indigenous peoples—Study and teaching—Canada. | LCSH: Reconciliation—Study and teaching—Canada. | LCSH: Curriculum planning—Canada.
Classification: LCC LC196.5.C2 D36 2024 | DDC 370.11/5—dc23

Legal Deposit: Fourth Quarter 2024
Library and Archives Canada

Printed in Canada

Production Team
Copy editing   Crystal Chan
Proofreading   Robbie McCaw
Typesetting   John van der Woude
Cover design   Benoit Deneault

Cover Image
Amber Bracken, World Press Photo of the Year, Kamloops Residential School Memorial, 2022.

We would like to thank the Dean of the Faculty of Education and Social Work, Yasmin Dean, for her financial support in relation to this book.

The University of Ottawa Press gratefully acknowledges the support extended to its publishing list by the Government of Canada, the Canada Council for the Arts, the Ontario Arts Council, the Federation for the Humanities and Social Sciences through the Scholarly Book Awards (ASPP) and the Social Sciences and Humanities Research Council, and by the University of Ottawa.

ONTARIO ARTS COUNCIL
CONSEIL DES ARTS DE L'ONTARIO
an Ontario government agency
un organisme du gouvernement de l'Ontario

Ontario

Canada Council   Conseil des arts
for the Arts   du Canada

Canada

uOttawa

Land Acknowledgement

Thompson Rivers University campuses are on the traditional lands of the Tk'emlúps te Secwépemc (Kamloops campus) and the T'exelc (Williams Lake campus) within Secwepemcúĺecw, the traditional and unceded territory of the Secwépemc. Our region also extends into the territories of the St'át'imc, Nlaka'pamux, Nuxalk, Tŝilhqot'in, Dakelh, and Syilx peoples.

FIGURE 1. Secwepemcúĺecw, looking east along the South Thompson River valley. *Source*: Gordon Leary.

In Your Canada—
A Thousand and Counting

Garry Gottfriedson

a dress, a red dress, a thousand more dresses
suspended from crucifixes

tribute to the Holy Trinity:
daughter, mother, grandmother

condemned by the church
concealed by the government

caught in black clouds weeping
thunder breaking sky blue

a single rainbow drops from heaven
bridging souls to something much higher

than the sins of mortal men
hell bent on killing brown women

as if hysterectomies, rape and murder
was not enough punishment

warranted by a civilized society
that honours genocide

all encapsulated by a single photo
a dress, a red dress, a thousand more dresses

FIGURE 2. Dangling.
Source: Amber Bracken.

About the Cover Photograph

The photograph was taken by Canadian photographer Amber Bracken for *The New York Times*, just days following the discovery of 215 unmarked graves at the Kamloops Indian Residential School. It won World Press Photo of the Year in 2022. The subject of this photo is the display that was installed by women of the Secwépemc Nation along the highway leading to the former Kamloops Indian Residential School. It commemorated the children who died at the school. Said Rena Effendi, global jury chair for the World Press Photo of the Year competition: "It is the kind of image that sears itself into your memory, it inspires a kind of sensory reaction. I could almost hear the quietness in this photograph, a quiet moment of global reckoning for the history of colonization, not only in Canada but around the world" (*The Guardian*, April 7, 2022). Amber Bracken identified that this photo showed the rainbow descending, seemingly to the ground, and touching the exact location of some of the unmarked graves of children who attended the Kamloops Indian Residential School (KIRS) between the years of 1896 and 1976. It is a poignant, single frame that speaks in a different way to the Truth and Reconciliation Commission's six Calls to Action titled "Missing Children and Burial Information."

We remain unclear about the number of children who attended KIRS as the Oblates of Mary Immaculate will not release this information to the Secwépemc Nation. The first half of our book's title, *Dangling in the Glimmer of Hope*, is a line from a poem written by Garry Gottfriedson. The line rings with power. The poem is from Garry's book *Bent Back Tongue*, a collection of poetry published by Caitlin Press in 2022.

A visceral response is provoked when taken together: the powerful photograph; the poetry Garry has written to express in words elements of this photograph; the line of poetry, "dangling in the glimmer of hope"; and the Calls to Action. This book is about hope.

Table of Contents[*]

---

*   Some authors have embedded poetry within a chapter. Some authors have stand-
     alone poetry. When a poem is embedded in the chapter, it is not listed in the Table of
     Contents; instead, you will find it in the List of Poems. When it is a stand-alone piece of
     writing, it is listed in the Table of Contents as well as in the List of Poems.

List of Poems

List of Figures

List of Tables

Foreword

Dorothy Cucw-la7 Christian

As an Indigenous/Secwépemc-Syilx scholar I read a lot of documents about reconciliation and decolonizing. Sometimes it's exhausting and sometimes it's exhilarating.

My Secwépemc name is Cucw-la7 and I am from the Splatsin community in Secwepemcúlecw, the unceded territories of the Secwépemc Nation. I often say, "My colonial name is Dorothy Christian and I'm not! Some priest bestowed this last name on my family." I am the eldest of ten, and nine of us are still living. I am a mother to one daughter and an Auntie, great-Auntie and great-great-Auntie to about 70 nieces, nephews, great-nieces and -nephews, and at least two great-great-nieces. I currently live, work, and play on the territories of my Coast Salish cousins, the Tsleil-Waututh, the Musqueam, and the Squamish Nations. At Simon Fraser University (SFU) I am in the role of associate director, Indigenous Policy, and Pedagogy in the Graduate Studies unit. I also sit as Elder/Auntie on the Equity, Diversity, and Inclusion Advisory Council at SFU and work closely with the offices of President Joy Johnson and Vice-President, People, Equity and Inclusion, Yabome Gilpin-Jackson. I am deeply entrenched in reconciliation and decolonizing and sometimes Indigenizing at the university, at many levels of engagement. I have been involved in so-called reconciliation work for over 30 years, long before "reconciliation," "decolonizing," and "Indigenizing" became buzz words in the academy. From my Indigenous/Secwépemc-Syilx perspective, my understanding of reconciliation is the same as that of Maria Campbell, who writes: "You cannot reconcile a relationship that never existed. We don't need any more sorrys.* We have closets full of *sorrys*. There is no word in Cree for Reconciliation. Only 'kwayskahstahsoowin' which means 'setting things right.' Restoring what is ours would set things right. Giving our land back would set things right" (personal communication, February 9, 2020). "Sorrys" do nothing if the same policies and practices that continue to demand and disrespect Indigenous peoples continue.

Two things I know for sure about reconciliation are:

One, the work is most effective when an Indigenous person and a "woke" non-Indigenous person work together to create places of true reconciliation and take meaningful action that actualizes in real change/transformation. The term "woke" to me means a settler person who is engaged and committed to their own growth and development in the sometimes uncomfortable process of unlearning and decolonizing practices on personal and professional levels. So many non-Indigenous people think that reconciliation work is only for Indigenous peoples.

Two, reconciliation is all about the lands of the original peoples within the geopolitical boundaries of this nation-state known as Canada. Settlers are afraid we want the land back. Subconsciously, they know the land was acquired through nefarious means! When you start pulling away all the layers of whatever conflict lies between Indigenous and settler peoples, at the very core is the land (Barker & Battell Lowman, 2015, p. 48). In 2011 I wrote a chapter, "Reconciling With the People and the Land?" in the Aboriginal Healing Foundation's book, *Cultivating Canada: Reconciliation through the Lens of Cultural Diversity* that speaks directly to some of the layers of issues which contribute to the need for settlers to wake up and "make things right" with the original peoples of these lands.

The editors, Garry Gottfriedson and Victoria Handford, invited me to write the foreword for this book, *Dangling in the Glimmer of Hope: Academic Action on Truth and Reconciliation*, I suspect because they are aware of my body of work in the area of reconciliation. I have known my Secwépemc brother Garry for over 30 years and he is a highly respected knowledge keeper, language speaker, storyteller, writer, poet, and scholar. I say the knowledge keepers are our professors and the land is our university. I have known Tory Handford for a short time, through academic conferences.

I was excited when they asked me to be a part of this anthology. The text is unique in so many ways. How often do you see poetry and creative

---

* As far as I know, there is no word for "reconciliation" in Secwepemctsín. I have not consulted language speakers for clarification.

writing next to academic analysis? How often do you see Indigenous and settler scholars from many different disciplines intimately engaged together in peeling away the accrued layers of colonial harm? How often do you read chapters written by non-Indigenous scholars who have a deep understanding of Indigenous/Secwépemc knowledge, and who are, with that knowledge, recommending how to enhance practices that will benefit the local Indigenous population? How often do you read revelations by settlers of colour that look deeply at how the Indigenous peoples were treated in their home country and then reflect deeper still on how that experience informs their relationships to the Indigenous peoples of where they now live?

This is the first text that I have read where Indigenous/Secwépemc and settler scholars are writing about their shared relational experiences as they co-exist on the lands of the local Indigenous/Tk'emlúps te Secwépemc peoples. It is particularly powerful because these are the lands where the finding of 215 unmarked graves of children was announced in May 2021. That significant historical marker blew apart the colonial narrative of these lands, which has bullied its way into the hearts and minds of non-Indigenous Canadians over centuries. The silent voices of the children opened the dialogue between Indigenous and settler peoples so that the *truth* of the Indigenous narrative is *finally* beginning to be heard.

The framework of this book sets out to address some of the 94 Calls to Action of the Truth and Reconciliation Commission, specifically related to language and culture, health, education, business, commemoration, and newcomers. The brilliance of the text below is that it brings together the academic mind, which always thinks it's so smart, and the creative mind, which is more tentative and more open to exploring new ways of seeing, hearing, and doing. As a reader, we weave in and out of graphics that touch our visual senses; we read poetry that touches the deeper part of our heart and spirit in nuanced ways; and we read the lived experiences of academics conscientiously engaging the mind to undo and unlearn.

The "truth" part of Truth and Reconciliation is shown in the chapters of this text. Because of space constraints, I only refer to two truth tellers who had my full attention as I read their chapters. Gloria Ramirez in Section 1 shares intimate details of her lived experience in her homelands and in the new lands she chose as her current home. She is a global Indigenous settler person striving to be a "good relative" and a good ally to the Secwépemc as she learns their/our language and cultural practices. Georgann Cope Watson's chapter in Section 2 is one of the most honest written accounts I have read from a white woman scholar. She talks about her white privilege and being raised in a society based on white supremacist ideology, but most importantly, Watson describes her unlearning and how she has moved into reconcili*action*; that is, into action in her personal and professional life. She is a living example of being a woke white settler. For certain, the damage of colonization cannot be healed by the colonized or the colonizer isolating themselves in separate corners. We do need privacy to do our personal healing; however, the harsh realities that were created through this process can only be undone and unlearned by both sides of the colonial coin working together in a kind, compassionate, and healing environment. This cultural interface, this place where we sit together, must be a safe place where discomfort is allowed. Together, we explore how to unlearn and learn; we learn how to be interrelated with all the beings in Secwepemcúĺecw, including the human beings.

Hope seems a trite word to use when referring to this body of work. The depth of engagement that is being displayed in the writing completed on the lands of Secwepemculu is profound. These individuals, some of whom are Indigenous and Secwepemc, or Indigenous and from other lands, and some of whom are non-Indigenous, are all scholars and creators. The work that occurred as they touched each other's lives speaks to something greater than hope. Their work together sets a strong foundation for the generations of Indigenous/Secwépemc and non-Indigenous settler peoples who will come after them. With this foundation, peaceful coexistence on these lands is a possibility. This anthology is an exemplar of regional work that can be shared with Indigenous and non-Indigenous communities across Canada.

With respect,
Dr. Dorothy Cucw-la7 Christian

Simon Fraser University, which is located on the unceded traditional territories of the Coast Salish peoples, including the səlilwətaɬ (Tsleil-Waututh), kʷikʷəʎəm (Kwikwetlem), Sḵwx̱wú7mesh Úxwumixw (Squamish) and xʷməθkʷəy̓əm (Musqueam) Nations.
Burnaby, British Columbia
January 30, 2024.

References

Battell Lowman, E., & Barker, A. J. (2015). *Settler: Identity and colonialism in 21st century Canada*. Fernwood Publishing.

Introduction

Garry Gottfriedson and Victoria Handford

Dangling in the Glimmer of Hope: Academic Action on Truth and Reconciliation invites and demonstrates actions by academics in relation to some of the Calls to Action of the Truth and Reconciliation Commission (TRC). It does this in two ways. Throughout you will find poetry, short stories, and children's stories. You will also encounter academic chapters. We hope you will find the mixing of personal and academic voices a challenge and engages you to consider what Truth and Reconciliation and the Calls to Action—require of each of us. These voices are used to engage both the head and the heart. Change needs the engagement of both to succeed.

The collection includes six chapters of varying styles and more than 10 poetry contributions, some of which are listed in the Table of Contents, and some of which are internal to the chapters themselves and are therefore listed only in the List of Poems. The actions that are addressed in this collection include "Language and Culture," "Health," "Education for Reconciliation," "Business and Reconciliation," "Commemoration," and "Newcomers to Canada," notwithstanding that the cover photo itself is a poignant, emotional representation of "Missing Children and Burial Information."

There are 22 titled sections in the Calls to Action. Much more must be done beyond this volume, and it needs to result in long-term change throughout the country. This book is only a beginning. More "coverage" would have been desirable; all the Calls to Action are important. However, Thompson Rivers University (TRU) is a medium-sized university, and the authors were all part of graduate programs in education. This department does not have 22 members. It is small. While more needs to be done, we appreciate the engagement of so many in such an important undertaking. This issue is one Indigenous people experience themselves. They are stretched far and wide, not able to meet the many critical needs in community, extended communities, and nationally. The engagement of Indigenous colleagues and knowledge keepers in this volume was and is a statement of generosity. What is remarkable is the commitment of eight members of this small department, who are also all stretched in many directions. These members ranged from a research chair with many years of experience to a first-year tenure-track member, to sessional faculty, to an administrative coordinator. Some have long publication profiles. For others, this is one of their first efforts at publication. This is what universities are! There are many voices. To address the struggles in Canada we need to engage all voices. All contribute value. We hope you will see the value in each author.

One of the aims of this book is to provoke real change. The Calls to Action, published in 2015, make it clear that colonial thinking and pandering to issues rather than addressing them must stop. To this end, we embrace the Indigenous values of all people. It is the voices of the many, aiming at change, that is going to make this country better for all. For "all" includes beginning, experienced, and expert academics. We invited all: those willing and able to invest the time and energy to learn and to, correspondingly, work. There was vulnerability for everyone in this process. By using the priorities of a university related to research and dissemination, we hope we will change the country! This work is academic, albeit also creative (ideally then—using both sides of the brain, and a level of personalization that is often not part of academic writing). It will take a total investment, including all brain capacity and emotional capacity, to do what needs to be done.

This collection is intended to be helpful, to stimulate creativity, and, most importantly, to encourage all to act according to their abilities, interests, and opportunities, on the actions demanded by the TRC Calls to Action. It may be useful in a college or university classroom. It may be useful for Indigenous communities. And it may inspire other works that expand on this concept. In the end, the goal remains the same—change. Change requires personal commitment. We hope we inspire commitment and actions. Tk'emlúps.

Storytelling and Change—Garry Gottfriedson

Storytelling is magical. I know this firsthand. I grew on the Tk'emlúps te Secwépemc in an era when there were no televisions or radios. Our form of entertainment came through the voice of my dad, an amazing story-teller. My mother was a great orator as well, but taught us through song and dance, which in my culture were based on stories. Not only this, but the Secwépemc culture is rich with stories.

So, I offer this story.

In the spirit of truth and reconciliation, the former dean of the Faculty of Education and Social Work (EDSW) at TRU, Dr. Airini, had created the first ever Secwépemc Cultural Advisor position to the dean. This position was meant to guide Dr. Airini and the faculty toward deeper understandings of the TRC, something no other university in Canada had done.

When I was hired in 2018 as the first Secwépemc Cultural Advisor to Dr. Airini, I wanted to address issues of the TRC's Calls to Action in a non-threatening way. So, I began telling stories of my people to the faculty, using Secwépemc storytelling to challenge this faculty to rise above the status quo. I wondered what the response would be, but quickly learned that the faculty members were drawn into the experience. And they wanted more.

During this time, I realized that TRU lacked an understanding of not only local Secwépemc culture but also of what Indigenization, decolonization, and reconcili*action* meant from an Indigenous perspective. Thus, the university was not actively engaged in addressing the TRC Calls to Action at any meaningful level. Clearly, TRU sits directly in the heart of the Secwépemc Nation, and discussions regarding Indigenous issues must include the Secwépemc world view and Secwépemc language. This inspired me to challenge TRU to respond to the TRC more actively.

Through storytelling, I offered faculty members insights into the Secwépemc world view and culture never before available at TRU. Then I helped faculty and staff understand the significance and importance of the TRC at deeper levels. At first, many faculty members were outright challenged since it meant examining their own stories, values, and beliefs as they heard firsthand experiences from an Indigenous point of view. Faculty members heard from survivors of the residential school system, learned about Canadian policies and politics specific to Indigenous peoples, probed into the rise of resistance by and the renewal of local First Nations. Faculty members explored important issues specific to the revival of language, culture, and identity, learned about the atrocity of murdered and missing Indigenous women and girls in Canada, and examined issues around racism and sexism toward Indigenous peoples and others, and the history and truth of the Kamloops Indian Residential School. The greatest learning was self-evaluation of Canadian society and its hidden histories from an Indigenous perspective.

EDSW shifted tremendously. This shift enticed the faculty to be more open to Indigenous world views and examine the context of hidden Canadian history, but more importantly, faculty examined themselves as they related to Indigenous peoples and views. This led the team to express their uneasiness with not knowing about Indigenous issues. As a community we explored how the silent listening and respectful presence found in a talking circle informs understanding. We learned through the principles of talking circle concepts that respect and freedom are true expressions that come from the heart. This also offered a safe process for open discussion of historical and current issues and events that affect First Nations, Inuit, and Métis people in Canada today.

We experienced Secwépemc ways of knowing by providing a safe space for each person to contribute and to discover their voice. The result enhanced the faculty's own experience.

In addition, EDSW was inspired to consider new program initiatives, and to revisit their course outlines, plans, and mission statements. Many revisions to course content included aspects of the TRC. Faculty chairs also took the inspiration a little further by revising their vision and mission statements so EDSW would be more aligned with the TRC.

In addition, a very significant sign of growth for EDSW was the addition of the Texw-téxtwt-ken re lleqmélt ("I will be a strong teacher") program. Assistant Teaching Professor and PhD candidate Roxane Letterlough from the St'at'imc Nation designed the Texw-téxtwt-ken re lleqmélt program, which was added to EDSW's core programming and offered further understanding of Indigenous methodology and approaches to Indigenous education. It also addressed key issues raised by the TRC specific to student retention and success. The program challenged the Faculty of Education's status quo, but the insights gained were rewarding.

EDSW continued its growth by offering more courses informed by Indigenous ways of knowing in their graduate programs in education. To mention some, Indigenous professors offered Learning from the Land (offered in all three seasons), Indigenous Methodology, Healing from the Land, Indigenous Pedagogies, Oral Traditions and Research, and Learning Through First Nations Literature.

Other successes heightened TRU's desire to address the TRC. These included the award-winning program created by Dr. Rod McCormick and Dr. Airini called the Knowledge Makers. This program supports Indigenous students in becoming excellent scholars and researchers. It promotes students' work through a published journal and is "dedicated to transforming universities by engaging Indigenous students across disciplines in research and publication" (Knowledge Makers, n.d.).

Other examples that address the TRC throughout TRU include the efforts made by Associate Professor and Canada Research Chair Dr. Shelly Johnson (Mukwa Musayett) toward decolonizing the university. The Faculty of Law has redesigned their entry programs by including law courses specific to the Secwépemc Nation in the first two years of study. Those courses expand student learning by teaching the historical, philosophical, and legal frameworks from the Secwépemc point of view. The Office of Indigenous Education works with all deans, faculties, and departments to assist with many aspects of the TRC Calls to Action, and helps with courses, curriculum, and programs to assist with decolonization efforts. The Office of Indigenous Education also runs The Coyote Project, whose mandate is to eliminate employment and educational gaps. This project works to further address issues around student retention and success university-wide. TRU has entered into a formal and legal partnership agreement with the Tk'emlúps te Secwépemc to ensure that protocols, educational needs, and respectful relationships are adhered to at the community and university levels. These are further examples of work that address the TRC Calls to Action. Although these efforts are great beginnings, TRU still has so much more work to do.

Understanding and Critical Thought—Victoria Handford

I am currently a professor and chair of the School of Education. I teach and research in areas of education leadership. I coordinated graduate programs in education for six years and have served on many committees. My favourite role at TRU is one-to-one supervision work with thesis and project students. I become part of student learning and a part of their lives. Learning is a shared adventure, of laughter, of togetherness, and of exploration. How lucky am I that I get to do this work!

I am originally from Ontario, a descendant of white settlers who arrived in Canada sometime in the 1700s. I was born and raised in London, Ontario. The city is located on the traditional lands of the Anishinabek, Haudenosaunee, Lūnaapéewak, and Attawandaron peoples, on lands connected with Treaty 7 and the Dish with One Spoon Wampum. I knew none of these names as a child, though I did have classmates who were from nearby First Nations communities.

In elementary school we learned First Nations history mainly as it related to periods of settlement, including reading, or being read, portions of *The Jesuit Relations*. We visited the site of Ste. Marie among the Hurons and could identify on a map the territories of those who were part of the Iroquois Confederacy. I could name some major Iroquois leaders such as Tecumseh and other Indigenous leaders, such as Dumont. I was mindful that without First Nations involvement in the War of 1812, Canada would not today be a country. In all cases, in elementary or secondary school, the emphasis was on the memorization of names, dates, events, and locations. So I was aware of the physical context but I was not educated in the cultures, languages, and traditions of Indigenous peoples.

An important experience for me during time I spent working at the Ontario College of Teachers (OCT) was serving as the program officer and staff lead for the accreditation of an Indigenous language instruction program in 2010 and 2011. I had led reviews of other Indigenous programs, but for this program, the OCT determined that continuing to have non-Indigenous people doing accreditation reviews of Indigenous programs was highly problematic. The five-day site visit with very knowledgeable and talented Indigenous language speakers from several Nations, bands, and language groups in Ontario was an awakening for me. I listened carefully to the conversations, hearing the strengths, concerns, and next steps as identified by those who knew the issues. As we moved into report writing my learning became ever deeper. The respect and admiration for the knowledge and intentions of those on the panel changed not only the report, but me. The report was well done, the feedback to the program was excellent, and the program was later fully accredited. I deeply respect those individuals who offered so much of themselves when I think about the issues Indigenous peoples face, and what it means to be in community.

My experiences at the OCT as well as experiences with First Nations in Yukon inspired me to explore. The importance of Indigenous issues is everywhere in Kamloops and invited deeper considerations. Our former dean, Airini, was such an encouraging colleague and advocate for action. Having Garry, Rod, Shelly (Mukwa Musayett), Natalie, Roxane, and Uncle Mike within or associated with our faculty provided more opportunities for me to learn. In the winter of 2021, I enrolled as a student in Garry's graduate course in Indigenous Literature. I soon recognized I was in the class of a master teacher. The discussions Garry facilitated were far more than an analysis of Indigenous literature. Garry invited students to explore out loud the issues that the literature revealed, the understandings and misunderstandings held, and the influences of these issues on education in Canada. The requirement to write creative assignments (short stories, poetry, etc.) challenged me to do something I had not done since high school (quite a few years ago!) I found considering the topics this way inviting. It also required me to have quite a personal, though still a beginner's, understanding of the issues.

In May 2021, the remains of 215 children were found on the grounds of the Kamloops Indian Residential School on the lands of the Tk'emlúps te Secwépemc Nation. At TRU, issues that might have remained as "we're working on them" status moved to "priority one." The need to "action" the Calls to Action was profound.

Developing the Collection—Garry's and Tory's Voices

Faculty and staff in graduate programs in education at TRU wanted to engage in meaningful learning in relation to our neighbours and friends whose ancestors have lived in Secwepemcúlecw for thousands of years. The only way we could be "in community" was to consciously demonstrate a lived commitment to the process of truth and reconciliation and engage in actions related to the Calls to Action. Academics write. So, learning and then using our academic voices in conversation and in writing to extend and articulate our learning was where we started. We quickly learned that a more "resonant" voice was needed. Garry helped us find that. Eventually we extended the workshop model into a writing community that was informed by friends within Secwepemcúlecw. And we took risks to broaden the range of our voices. The results became this book.

This approach to the TRC's Calls to Action was, in a sense, a weaving our academic identities with new and fresh approaches, including storytelling and poetry. This collection is our story.

The writing process was part of an intensive eight-week dialogue of professional development in which the writers researched an area of interest based on the TRC's Calls to Action. Each week, the participants engaged in a two-hour session led by Garry, discussing Indigenous issues, historical misrepresentations, and work within the university and our classrooms that enabled deeper understanding of Canada and its histories. Garry included workshops about three genres of creative writing: poetry, writing children's stories, and short story writing, styles of writing not used as frequently by researchers in higher education. It was an effort to bridge the academic side of the brain and the creative side of the brain, producing both more personal—and richer—writing. And it worked! Many participants chose to include one of these genres as a writing style. Some combined these styles within a research article. Others wrote opinion pieces. Through writing and learning from firsthand experience of the historical, political, and oppressive conflict between Canada and Indigenous peoples, the participants better understood the Calls to Action.

We extended the eight-week dialogue and held a two-day writing retreat at a local Indigenous resort. Three Elders and several Indigenous colleagues participated. One Indigenous colleague, Rod McCormick, contributed a chapter to this volume. Having these individuals offer their voices and insights to each author in a process that invited many voices and perspectives was of enormous value. It was a cultural fact-checking. Dialogue led to deeper understanding. Friendships were formed. Elder Mike stated at the end of our two-day event: "Please don't let this be the end of this. Work until you have finished the book. Then keep working. This is important."

While the faculty could write academically, one important way in which they demonstrated action was engaging in the creative writing that was less familiar for most academics. It may have been that the creative process was closer to the bone. This challenged the participants to dig deeply into their understanding of Indigenous issues in a balanced, non-threatening way and to give critical thought to the topic. Many authors took the risk of writing outside their area of academic expertise. This is how we need to view our histories and Canada—with new eyes, with new voices.

As the articles, creative works, and the book emerged, we began looking for an organizational framework. We determined that using the Calls to Action was completely appropriate for this book. There are 94 specific calls within the Calls to Action, divided into 22 categories. Authors had responded to 6 of the 22 main categories in the Calls to Action. Each section contains a mix of academic and creative writing, with some authors including poetry or a story within their article.

The voice of each author is presented through their writing in one of the six sections, in whatever style(s) they have selected. While contributions may address components of multiple Calls to Action from a variety of overall themes, we have placed all that an author has written in the one section that seems to be the best overall fit. Each author is on their own journey, but together, we are on one journey as a department—and as a country. Experience in the academy, with publishing, and with the Calls to Action varied considerably. This is one of the strengths of the book; the voices differ.

We are thankful for each author who dared to put pen to paper. It is a risk. We are better for them taking that risk.

The Elders

FIGURE 3. The three Elders spent two days offering us their wisdom at our retreat; *left to right*: Minnie Grinder Kenoras, Mike Arnouse, and Flora Sampson.
Source: Victoria Handford.

They invested time and took the energy to speak to the group and individuals with intention. The Elders were central to our process. We have included very brief biographies which Garry Gottfriedson and Natalie Clark gathered.

Uncle Mike Arnouse is a Secwépemc Elder from the Adams Lake community. He has been an Elder on the campus of Thompson Rivers University for more than 20 years.

He is a helper who believes in learning from one another. He appreciates the opportunities to meet and talk with students, staff, and faculty, as we all can learn from each other. He shares his knowledge freely. He makes note that knowledge, however, has been hidden from his people for so long.

Mike believes that everything we learn and share about the medicines, animals, and stories is for the future generation. The colonization of our culture and the copyrights to knowledge systems are a hindrance to carrying the knowledge of the history of Secwepemcúlecw and Cḱuḻtns re Secwepemc (way of life).

Knowledge is best passed through relationships and talking to one another. Mike invites people to sit and talk with him anytime that he is on campus. Have tea and chat. Be yourself and have a heart-to-heart. Build relationships and friendship and family.

Elder Minnie Grinder Kenoras is a Secwépemc Elder who is passionate about transferring her significant traditional Indigenous knowledge and lived experience to our younger generation. She facilitates girls' groups with Dr. Natalie Clark, holds workshops, and recently held seasonal camps for hunting, foraging, and berry picking and gathering. She has been working on preserving her vast knowledge through a series of videos and a robust social media presence to revitalize Secwépemc ways of knowing, being, and learning. She is an advocate of revitalizing culture as a way of caring for children, and by extension, the community, to promote healing and self-identity by raising up women and girls through experiential, traditional crafts, sustenance, and ceremony.

Elder Flora Sampson was deeply rooted in Secwépemc cḱuḻtns (Secwépemc culture) and Secwepemctsín (Secwépemc language), despite having attended the Kamloops Indian Residential School for many years. She was a fluent speaker, educator, and highly respected Knowledge Keeper. Flora dedicated her life to the preservation of Secwepemctsín and Secwépemc culture, working endlessly to ensure that her knowledge was passed on. She was an amazing singer and dancer. She was also a strong activist fighting for the rights of the Secwépemc, especially those related to land and water. Elder Flora passed to the spirit world in the fall of 2022. She will be deeply missed by all who knew her.

Indigenous Colleagues

Natalie Clark and Rod McCormick generously engaged with each of us for two days and had multiple writing discussions with us later. The journey to reconciliation is a path with many steps, and much dialogue. We are so grateful for their involvement in this project.

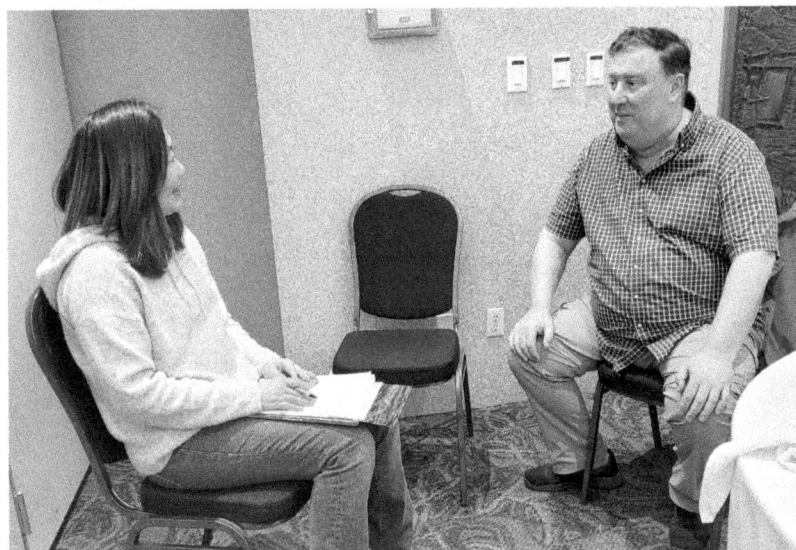

TOP: **FIGURE 4.** Natalie Clark in conversation with Fred Schaub.
ABOVE: **FIGURE 5.** Rod McCormick in conversation with Patricia Liu Baergen.
Source: Victoria Handford.

Natalie Clark is a professor in the School of Social Work and Human Service at Thompson Rivers University. Her practice as a social worker includes work as a clinical supervisor, educator, and counsellor specializing in violence and trauma as well as a girls' group facilitator for Indigenous girls.

Rod McCormick is an Indigenous health researcher and clinician. His nation is Kanien'kehá:ka (Mohawk). He lives on reserve in his partner's home community of Tk'emlúps te Secwépemc. Rod's professional training and experience is in counselling psychology and in Indigenous mental health. His research focuses on community capacity building in Indigenous mental health and research as well as the reclamation of traditional forms of healing.

References

Knowledge Makers. (n.d.). About Knowledge Makers. TruBox. https://knowledge makerstest.trubox.ca/about

LANGUAGE AND CULTURE CALLS TO ACTION

The Truth and Reconciliation Commission (2015, p. 2) made five Calls to Action for language and culture. Issues named as priorities for change in relation to language and culture in the Calls to Action are as follows:

13. We call upon the federal government to acknowledge that Aboriginal rights include Aboriginal language rights.
14. We call upon the federal government to enact an Aboriginal Languages Act that incorporates the following principles:
    i. Aboriginal languages are a fundamental and valued element of Canadian culture and society, and there is an urgency to preserve them.
    ii. Aboriginal language rights are reinforced by the Treaties.
    iii. The federal government has a responsibility to provide sufficient funds for Aboriginal-language revitalization and preservation.
    iv. The preservation, revitalization, and strengthening of Aboriginal languages and cultures are best managed by Aboriginal people and communities.
    v. Funding for Aboriginal language initiatives must reflect the diversity of Aboriginal languages.
15. We call upon the federal government to appoint, in consultation with Aboriginal groups, an Aboriginal

Languages Commissioner. The commissioner should help promote Aboriginal languages and report on the adequacy of federal funding of Aboriginal-languages initiatives.

16. We call upon post-secondary institutions to create university and college degree and diploma programs in Aboriginal languages.

17. We call upon all levels of government to enable residential school Survivors and their families to reclaim names changes by the residential school system by waiving administrative costs for a period of five years for the name-change process and the revision of official identity documents, such as birth certificates, passports, driver's licences, health cares, and social insurance numbers.

References

Truth and Reconciliation Commission of Canada. (2015). *Truth and Reconciliation Commission of Canada: Calls to Action*. https://ehprnh2mwo3.exactdn.com/wp-content/uploads/2021/01/Calls_to_Action_English2.pdf

Returning from School

Garry Gottfriedson

when you return from KIRS
bruised and blue
optimism
barely
surviving
nonetheless, alive
calling your spirit
home
reminding you
your family still stands firm
open to the sun
waiting to blanket you
sage smoke adrift
rising from our cupped hands
sweeping a path
for your wondering feet
guided back to us
where you belong
where our people have always belonged in
Secwepemcúlecw

remember our strength,
broken as it may be,
arises from the sage smoke and dust

of those who walked
the same path as us
generations before
teaching us to dig deeply
into the sweetness of this land
baring our roots
tracking the hoofprints of tsi7 – the deer
and making our way to setétkwe – the river
tossing salmon skeletons
back into the water
for these elements
carry the celebration of those
who once lived among us
and have kept us resilient
despite destructive attempts to
expunge ckuĺtns – our way of being
and when you are
crazy with confusion
your returning
signals
tsqelmucwílc – your return to becoming
    human
forever more

FIGURE 1.1. Garry
Gottfriedson by the fire.
Source: Victoria Handford.

Disrupting Colonial Practices through Indigenous Language Learning and Research

Gloria Ramirez

Abstract

In this chapter, I examine my journey of collaboration with Secwépemc educators, Elders, fluent Secwepemctsín speakers, tselexmemin (knowledge keepers), and community members involved in Secwepemctsín revitalization. I engage in structured reflexivity to trace what this transformative experience has taught me about Indigenous research paradigms, culturally appropriate research with Secwépemc communities, and Secwépemc values and world views. I also reflect on how learning an Indigenous language and making space for it is an act of resistance to colonial practices. I draw primarily on knowledge written and spoken by Secwépemc scholars, Elders, and knowledge keepers. To honour different ways of expression and knowledge construction, I have structured this piece to blend academic discourse, poetry, narratives, and storytelling. To honour Secwepemctsín and make space for it, I embed words from the language as often as possible.

FIGURE 1.2. Considering the writing; *left to right*: Gloria Ramirez, Elder Minnie Grinder Kenoras, and Joanne (Manuel) Buffalo (daughter of Minnie).
Source: Victoria Handford.

For educators and researchers, decolonization is about disrupting the Eurocentric discourses, structures, and practices that permeate teaching, learning, and research. It is about listening to Indigenous voices; it is about understanding and valuing Indigenous peoples' world views; it is about making space for Indigenous knowledges and praxis. Scholars have long been required to adhere to the traditional structure and style of academic writing, which was inspired by the so-called scientific method. One of the central tenets of this convention is objectivity, which is interpreted as a sign of intellectual maturity. There is no space for feelings, just facts and logical reasoning. My collaborations with Secwépemc people and Indigenous scholars have led me to question this. Who established such norms? Whose values, belief systems, and paradigms do these conventions represent, and why? When is it appropriate to conform to it, and when is it not? These conventions privilege Eurocentric ways of thinking about knowledge transmission. As such, I wonder if this imposition is an example of colonialism in the academy.

Inevitably, these reflections lead to other questions: What is colonialism? How does it manifest among Indigenous peoples? How does it manifest among non-Indigenous peoples? How does it manifest in academic life? The following poem provides some answers.

Colonialism

> Take away
> Rob
> Impose
> Erase
> > Land
> > Identity
> > Language
> > Culture
>
> Measure
> > Time
> > Restrict
> > Confine
> > > Life
> > > Knowledge
> > > Blood quantum
> > > People
>
> Colonialism
> The Indian Act

As I recognized different manifestations of colonialism, I found I could move to decolonize, to make space for diverse ways of thinking, saying, writing, and doing. I could attempt to make space for diverse voices and ways of being. I could be disrupting, not conforming.

To decolonize my academic and research praxis, I have let this chapter unfold in unconventional ways. It blends academic writing with other forms of expression such as storytelling and poetry.

This blend welcomes all the dimensions of my being—my emotions, my intellect, my spiritual realm. Traditional formats fragment, compartmentalize, and restrict. They would not allow for a holistic exploration of my experiences of collaborating with Secwépemc educators, Elders, fluent Secwepemctsín speakers, tselexmemin (knowledge keepers), and community members involved in Secwepemctsín revitalization. Using only traditional academic writing structures would mean having to numb parts of myself, but if I want to understand Secwépemc and other Indigenous world views, I cannot numb my feelings. I need to enter their space with all my being. This is not to deny a place for traditional academic writing and research report structures. There is indeed a place for that form of research and writing, and I step into that space as well when required. However, the context and holistic nature of the work presented here requires a format that welcomes subjectivity and emotions because, as wisely stated by Gordon Tomma, cultural interpreter at Quaaout Lodge, "You need the feeling before the healing" (personal communication, April 8, 2022). Poetry and narrative accounts provide space for feelings and emotions.

The reflections I share here are influenced by my life experiences prior to arriving in Secwepemcúĺecw and during the 13 years I have lived on this unceded territory. The Secwépemc have shaped who I am, and what I have come to understand about colonialism, Secwepemctsín revitalization as a form of decolonization, and Secwépemc research protocols. Thus, I will briefly share some aspects of my social location by exploring my Colombian roots. My arrival in Secwepemcúĺecw marked my awakening to the realities of colonialism and I became conscious of my own involvement in the Colombian and Canadian colonial schemes. I will reflect on my experience learning Secwepemctsín and my academic collaborations with Secwépemc communities to work toward revitalizing Secwepemctsín. The purpose of these structured reflections is to bring to the surface learnings about the Secwépemc culture, values, world views, and research paradigms.

My Social Location/My Roots

I was born in the Andean region of Colombia and lived on a farm for the first five years of my life. I know now that the first inhabitants of the land where I was born were the Indigenous peoples called the Tahamí, one of the groups from the Chibcha family. The Tahamí were peaceful people dedicated to agricultural activities, cultivating mainly corn, cotton, fruit, and beans (López, 1968). They also fished and mined gold from nearby rivers. They made containers of clay and weaved and dyed natural fibres to make clothing and other garments (López, 1968). Skilled merchants, they travelled by foot along the central and western Andean Mountain ranges to exchange agricultural products, cotton, and woven garments (Sistema Nacional de Información Cultural, n.d.). This history was absent from the social studies curriculum during my schooling. Instead, I learned about Captain Antonio Gomez de Castro, the Spaniard who is credited with founding El Santuario, the town where I grew up. He and his heirs were honoured every year, while the ancestral occupants of the land were ignored, erased from existence and from history. The name "El Santuario" means sanctuary, and according to historical accounts (*El Santuario, Antioquia: Capital agrícola de Antioquia*, n.d.) it is so named because it was a sanctuary of an Indigenous deity, which was replaced upon colonization by a sanctuary for the virgin of Chiquinquirá.

Unaware of my own distant Indigenous heritage, I saw Indigenous peoples through the lens portrayed in books, museums, and documentaries as exotic others. Theirs was a world distant from mine. In my journey to decolonize my personal history, I have been investigating the limited documentation available to learn about the Tahamí. It is still a mystery what Indigenous group my great-grandmother belonged to; she is merely identified in genealogical documentation as "la india," "the Indian." Circumstantial evidence suggests she was Tahamí, but without concrete evidence, this remains speculation.

My parents, Jesus Antonio Ramírez Arcila and María Belarmina Gómez Orozco, carry a centuries-long legacy of farming, only interrupted in my generation. I, like my 13 siblings, turned my back on farming to pursue education and prosperity. This education indoctrinated me in Colombian society's deep-rooted colonial mentality, which belittled Indigenous religions, world views, and ways of being. Fervent Catholics, my parents disregarded other faiths and religions, considering Indigenous spirituality as superstitious practices without value, and Indigenous peoples as in need of salvation through evangelization. Not surprisingly, I used to see assimilation as the ideal form of social integration.

Only in 1991 did Colombia's constitution recognize the fundamental rights of Indigenous peoples in the country. Through several articles (*Colombia's Constitution of 1991 with Amendments through 2015*, 2015), it recognizes cultural (Article 68), linguistic, (Article 10), territorial (Articles 63 and 72), educational (Article 68), political jurisdiction (Articles 246, 287, and 329), participation rights (Article 329), and the obligation of the state to protect Indigenous peoples' cultural assets (Article 8). Article 10 recognizes the languages and dialects of the ethnic groups as official languages within their territories and mandates bilingual education for students in their Indigenous language and Spanish. Article 68 mandates that education should respect and develop Indigenous peoples' cultural identity. The right to their land is also recognized in the constitution. For example, Article 63 states that the communal lands of ethnic groups and reservation lands cannot be taken away. Colombia's constitution of 1991 was the first step taken toward awaking from centuries of colonial apathy. However, these constitutional rights are constantly violated when Colombian and Indigenous peoples are violently displaced and murdered by armed groups representing financial interests. When Colombia was just starting to awake from centuries of colonial unconsciousness, Indian residential schools were still operating in Canada.

Awakening to the Truth

I engage in Secwepemctsín revitalization and structured reflection because, as stated by survivors of residential schools, it is my responsibility as a Canadian:

> Whether one is First Nations, Inuit, Métis, a descendant of European settlers, a member of a minority group that suffered historical discrimination in Canada, or a new Canadian, we all inherit both the benefits and obligations of Canada. We are all Treaty people who share responsibility for taking action on reconciliation. (Truth and Reconciliation Commission of Canada, 2015, p. 12)

The journey toward reconciliation must start with finding and telling the truth. Guided by Secwépemc research paradigms, this search started with me examining my own lived experiences before arriving in Secwepemcúlecw and during the years I have been here:

> S-tcúcmenstem is when we look inside of ourselves, to search for meaning. This is how we understand research. To be a researcher is to seek truth. That truth must benefit someone else, so it must be accurate, honest, and come from a good place of values and practices. We learn through research. (Gottfriedson et al., 2022, p. 1)

What is Truth?

> A forest mirrored on a lake
> the sun shining through the clouds
> embers after a fire
> What is truth?
> The broken heart of a mother
> the loneliness of a child
> bones rattling on the ground
> What is truth?

The salty water of the sea
the grinding taste of sand
bitterness of almond seeds

What is truth?
The moon moving the tides
wave crashing on the rock
wind sculpting the reef
What is truth?
The pins on the tongue
the scalding water on the skin
        for speaking the language

Arriving in Secwepemcúlecw

Oh, oh, ooh, ohiao, ohiao, ohia, ohia, ohia, ohia, ha io*
I pedal across the city; I hear distant drums
Oh, oh, ooh, ohiao, ohiao, ohia, ohia, ohia, ohia, ha io
I pedal to drumbeats; They set my direction
Oh, oh, ooh, ohiao, ohiao, ohia, ohia, ohia, ohia, ha io
My heart pounds loudly; I pedal fast; the drumbeats grow louder
Oh, oh, ooh, ohiao, ohiao, ohia, ohia, ohia, ohia, ha io

I arrive to a round structure bursting with people
Women wearing dresses with jingles, men wearing colourful
    arrangements of feathers,
regalia I am told.
The sun shining at 39°c degrees bathes my body in sweat
It is July 31st, 2009, my third day in Kamloops, Tk'emlúps.
People in regalia dance, circles of men drum and sing; the master
    of ceremony comments, jokes, laughs; the audience claps and
    cheers, the atmosphere is festive,
a Powwow I am informed.
This was my first interaction with the Secwépemc; my introduction
    to their culture.
Oh, ooh, ohiaao, ohiaao, ohia, ohiaao, ho, ho

---

*   When reading this part, put the words to the tune of the Secwépemc welcome song (go
    to https://www.youtube.com/watch?v=Vqf7IPuj7gw to listen to the song).

Living in Secwepemcúĺecw has been a transformative life experience. It has awakened me to the realities of colonialism. It has taught me about a unique, rich, ancestral culture, the Secwépemc. It has taught me to see the world in a different way. It has sparked my curiosity to learn about my own ancestral culture. It has taught me about the devastating effects of residential schools.

Numbers

150,000 broken souls,
        crying in darkness,
        shivering,
        sweating
        residential school children.

6,000 truth tellers,
        pounding hearts,
        clenching fists,
        grinding teeth
        survivors!

6,750 statements,
        unsettling,
        demanding,
        remembering
         survivors,
         families

215 clamours for justice,
        hidden,
        silenced,
        earthquake news,
        unmarked graves,
        Tk'emlúps.

93 testimonials of abuse,
        emotional,
        verbal,
        sexual,

           volatile,
           unmarked graves,
           Williams Lake.

751 booming voices,
        bones,
        rattling
        truth,
        unmarked graves,
        Saskatchewan.

5 million documents
        hiding truth,
        covering evil,
        justifying pain,
        misleading citizens,
        creating propaganda,
        Canadian government.

40 million Canadians
        frozen,
        confused,
        dismissive,
        heartbroken,
        enraged,
        in line to act,
        Canada.

Learning Secwepemctsín and Collaborating in its Revitalization

Secwepemctsín reflects the diversity of Secwépemc people. According to Ignace & Ignace (2017), Secwepemctsín has two dialects (Eastern and Western), with the Eastern dialect spoken by communities located east of Kamloops. These include Adams Lake, Neskonlith, Little Shuswap, Enderby, and Invermere. The Western dialect is spoken by communities in Kamloops and west, north, and northwest of Kamloops. Some researchers (e.g., Gottfriedson et al., 2022) identify three distinct dialects: Eastern, Western, and Northern, with the Western and Northern dialects being close to each other. The differences across dialects are minor, so speakers of each dialect can understand each other easily. I first started learning the Western dialect in 2010, soon after I arrived in Secwepemcúlecw, through classes offered in the community. In 2013, I was invited to collaborate with the Secwepemctsín team at the Sk'elep School of Excellence. The team included the school principal, fluent Elders, knowledge keepers, and teachers. This collaboration involved teacher mentoring, curriculum development, and research. This marked my real initiation to Secwépemc culture.

An extensive body of research and theory discusses the interconnections between language and culture and how language encodes teachings, values, ways of thinking and understanding of the wisdom and knowledge of the world (e.g., Chiblow & Meighan, 2022; Crystal, 2010; Davis, 2009; Harrison, 2007; Risager, 2006). As such, cultural characteristics and Secwépemc values are embedded in Secwepemctsín. For example, fishing with a scoop net was an important activity for the Secwépemc and its importance is reflected in a specialized vocabulary. Secwepemctsín, unlike English, has a special word for this: *yéwu*. Like other Indigenous languages, Secwepemctsín has built-in devices of grammar that help keep track of how to observe, make sense of, and communicate what the Secwépemc know of their social and natural universe and its interactions and interrelations.

Learning a language, building meaningful relationships with people, and learning about their culture requires intention and significant time investment. Over the past seven years I have been immersed in Secwépemc language and culture by collaborating with Eastern and Northern communities on community-based Secwepemctsín curriculum development, teacher mentoring, and intergenerational language learning. Following a community-based participatory model, I am collaborating in multi-layered ways, including as a student, mentor, mentee, and researcher. Above all, I am a constant learner. I participate in about 10 hours of Secwepemctsín classes per week and take advantage of any other learning opportunities (e.g., an ethnobotany course through Simon Fraser University and workshops/seminars/presentations by Secwépemc scholars and knowledge keepers). In addition, I interact regularly with fluent Elders, teachers, apprentices, knowledge keepers, and other community members engaged with Secwepemctsín revitalization. I also participate in community events whenever I am invited and available.

Below, I reflect on some key learnings I have obtained about Secwépemc culture through learning Secwepemctsín and collaborating with Secwépemc communities. These learnings include the strong connections with the land, the importance of kinship, the values of respect and humility, and the concept of relational accountability and responsibility.

Strong Connections with the Land

As Garry Gottfriedson said during our Indigenous Writing, Learning and Reconciliation seminar, "Everything I know about Secwépemc culture derives from the land" (personal communication, January 31, 2022). Secwépemc people are intimately connected to *tmicw* (the land), which is a comprehensive term relating not just to the soil or the ground, but also to all the things on it including sentient and non-sentient beings. Tmicw is the first teacher for the Secwépemc, the one that provides guidance on how to live, be, and learn.

> *Tmicw* is not about real estate or private property. It is about Secwépemc land in all its dimensions: It is the land of their ancestors experienced and marked out for them, and it comprises the living creatures in their land in their relations to humans, as well as the way that this land spoke back to countless generations of their ancestors who passed down their remembrances and the way that it continues to speak back to them. (Ignace & Ignace, 2017, p. 3)

The respect for tmicw emerges in the way the Secwépemc relate to it. I witnessed this myself during an ethnobotany field trip in the spring of 2021. Before proceeding to root digging, we respectfully made an offer to tmicw, asked for permission to dig out the roots, and thanked it for giving us food. This cultural protocol is an embodiment of the Secwépemc value of humans humbling themselves to nature, relating to it not as the masters with rights over it, but as servants of it. Congruent with this value, and like many Indigenous peoples around the world, the Secwépemc revere tmicw and see themselves as guardians of it. They practice sustainable resource management. Only portions of a plant are harvested, making sure the plant retains its capacity to regenerate. For example, when harvesting bark from cedar trees for basketry and other artisanal objects, attention is given to not removing more than a third of the tree's circumference (Turner et al., 2000). During the ethnobotany field trip, the participants strategically selected plants for root digging, with sustainability and preservation in mind.

For the Secwépemc, knowledge about plants is closely tied with cultural practices (e.g., harvesting for medicinal purposes and ceremonies). Knowledge about and management of plants and animal resources is traditionally distinct for men and women (Turner et al., 2000). Careful observation of tmicw experimentation over millennia provided knowledge and wisdom on the life cycle of different species, when and how to harvest in a respectful and sustainable way—

> seasonal signals such as position and size of snow patches on the mountains, or the arrival of the first snow in the fall; relative numbers of particular birds in a given location; flowering of certain plants; and productivity of certain berries: all of these provide indicators for people to know when to expect a salmon run, when the clams are ready to be dug, or when particular roots are ready for harvesting. (Turner, 1997 as cited in Turner et al., 2000, p. 1279)

Many Secwépemc words and expressions reveal their connection with the land. For example, the traditional way to ask a person's age in Secwepemctsín is *kwinc re7 swuct?* This literally means "How many winters did you pass?" (Elder M. Arnouse, personal communication, 2012; Elder L. Williams, Adams Lake Indian Band, personal communication, 2022). This connection is also reflected in how many months of the year are identified with what is happening on the land and the activities corresponding to it. March is Pellsqépts, which means "spring winds;" April is Pesll7éwten, which means "melting month;" May is Pell7é7llqten, which means "digging roots months;" July is Pelltqwelq̓wélt, which means "getting ripe month;" August is Pesqelglélȼen, which means "many salmon month;" September is Pelltemllík̓, which means "spawned out salmon month."

The importance of tmicw is also revealed in naming practices. Many women are given names containing the morpheme *ekwe*, which is used in words related to water. Others are named after animals (e.g., *Spi7uy* = bird), natural phenomena (e.g., *tseqtsq̓em* = thunder), places, and so on. Moreover, lexical suffixes categorize life forms, ascribe bodily forms into the landscape as geographic features, place names, and anatomy (Ignace, 2022). For example, the word *q̓wemtsín* (beach) contains the suffix "-tsín," which relates to mouth or edge.

The Importance of Kinship and Relational Accountability

In Secwépemc culture, as in many other cultures, traditional introductions begin with the family, starting with the grandparents, followed by parents, siblings, and children. This highlights the central role of kinship, which is also related to relational accountability (to be examined later). The vocabulary relating to family is extensive and sophisticated. It captures nuances related to different sides of the family and gender. The following, non-exhaustive, list illustrates this point by showing the specialized terminology for family members which, by comparison, does not exist in English:

qetsk = older brother
síntse = younger brother
kic = older sister
tsétse = younger sister
úq̓wi = sibling/cousin of the same sex
smé7ste = sibling/cousin of the opposite sex
qe7tse7éy'e = stepfather
ke7ce7éy'e = stepmother
tíkwe7 = aunt (father's sister)
túṁe = aunt (mother's sister)
síse7 = uncle (mother's brother)
méqse7 = uncle (father's brother)
s7ét.ste = brother or sister-in-law (opposite sex)
úq̓wiyéws = brother or sister-in-law (same sex)
lltsetsék = mother-in-law
sexéx7e = father-in-law
snek̓llcw = son-in-law
sépe = daughter-in-law
tsqwétsten = elder extended relatives (e.g., siblings)
sc7ítemc = elder relatives (e.g., elder brother or sister)
kyé7e = grandmother
qné7e = great grandmother

The many words used to refer to different family members in Secwepemctsín may reflect the prominence that Secwépemc culture gives to family and kinship. However, family relations are just one aspect of *xexwéyt ren kẇséseltkten* (all my relations). The concept relates to the interconnectedness of what in the English language is called "species," but also to the land itself. Everything on the land is sentient and speaks back. Humans, thus, must be and stay accountable (Ignace, 2022).

Through xwexwéyt ren kẇséseltkten, the Secwépemc practice reciprocal and relational accountability among all sentient beings on the land (including humans). This is part of Secwépemc ontology. Billy (2009, p. 17) describes this aspect of Secwépemc world view as follows: "Secwépemc ontology (world view) is grounded in the right relationship between people and the natural world. Traditional Secwépemc way of life was based on the land."

Relational accountability manifests in several ways in Secwépemc culture. Making offerings to the land, asking permission, and giving thanks before harvesting, fishing, and hunting, are ways the Secwépemc embody reciprocity and reciprocal accountability toward the land. Secwépemc Elders often remind us of this practice: "the food we eat each morning saves us. When we greet the sun, drink water, eat food, we think of the Creator" (Elder M. Arnouse, personal communication, April 8, 2022). He and other Elders (e.g., M. Kenoras, personal communication, April 8, 2022) constantly remind us of the importance of thinking carefully about our actions because they will affect us, others, the land, and the seven generations ahead. In a concentric organization of relationships, the Creator is at the centre, then the children, then the females and the mothers, then the Elders, then the protectors of the circle (Elder M. Arnouse, personal communication, April 8, 2022). Relational accountability manifests also through collaboration, through helping each other. As such, Secwépemc research guideline five states: "Me7 élkstwecw-kt ell c7ú7sten-kt (We will work in partnership)" (Gottfriedson et al., 2022, p. 5).

The Importance of Humility and Respect

Humility and respect are values at the core of Secwépemc culture, and I was introduced to them early in my collaborations with Secwépemc educators. The following story depicts the moment in the fall of 2013 when I was taught about humility by Elder Flora Sampson while collaborating on a project at Sk'elep School of Excellence. We (the Sk'elep Secwepemctsín team and I) had been working on creating picture books in Secwepemctsín using vocabulary from the thematic lessons we had created for the Secwepemctsín teacher. Full of excitement and pride, I showed kyé7e Flora the text for the picture book I was working on. The topic was parts of the body, and it was aimed at primary school children just learning the language. Thinking of building self-esteem along with teaching the language, I prepared the following text to be translated into Secwepemctsín:

Here are my eyes, they are beautiful, I love my eyes.
Here is my nose, it is beautiful, I love my nose.
Here is my mouth, it is beautiful, I love my mouth.

Here are my ears, my ears are beautiful, I love my ears.
Here are my hands, my hands are beautiful, I love my hands.

kyé7e Flora looked at me, displeased, and said: "That doesn't make sense!" Perplexed, I asked: "What do you mean?" "We don't say that," she responded. I eagerly proceeded to explain my good intentions: how I was trying to take this opportunity to build children's self-confidence and pride for how they looked. She was not persuaded and emphasized that it was wrong, that in Secwépemc culture they do not talk about themselves like that. "You don't say I am beautiful, or my eyes are beautiful," she emphasized. I finally understood what she was telling me. In Secwépemc culture, humility is highly valued; you are not supposed to praise yourself in any way. The text I had written was contrary to that value. In Secwépemc culture you should humble yourself to each other, to animals, to nature.

The value of *eyentwécw*, respect for one another, guides many aspects of the Secwépemc life. As examined earlier, it is embodied in the way they relate to tmicw and all the things in it, to each other, and to those still to be born. This value is reflected in the Secwépemc research ethics guidelines, which begin with the following statement:

E élkstwecw-et, me7 clecéllt se-kt, me7 teknémete xweyxwéyt t e stem, le7 en tsutcwíye, ta7e me7s xenestém, tústep, e yews kestwílcste re stem me7 le7es re s-w7ecs re tellqelmúcw.

When we work together, we have a good mind and we are kindhearted, to protect everything, and we must behave properly, to do no harm, damage or cause destruction for those yet to be born. (Gottfriedson et al., 2022, p. 1)

Beginning the research guidelines with this statement highlights the importance of this value; it makes it central to any research activity. The guidelines recognize the value of ancestors, Elders, and knowledge keepers in the creation and transmission of knowledge, thus emphasizing that earning academic credentials are just one way of acquiring knowledge. More directly, several Secwépemc research principles reflect the value of respect:

Principle 1. Me7 eyéstem re Secwépemc re s-tselxméms. We will respect Secwépemc knowledge.
Principle 3. Me7 secwentwécw. We will honour each other.
Principle 4. Wel me7 yews re tselxméms-kuc, ta7e me7 s-kwéctels tri7-k swet. We will respect equality in knowledge. (2022, p. 5)

The Secwépemc language encodes humility and respect in several ways. Reduplication, a grammatical feature of the language, is one way. In Northern and Western Secwepemctsín, reduplication is used to show politeness (Ignace & Ignace, 2017); for example, when talking to an Elder (e.g., saying *nens-ke* = I go, instead of *nes-ke*). Also, to show humility, the diminutive form of the verb is used (Ignace, 2022).

Secwépemc cultural values are traditionally transmitted from generation to generation through stories. I close this section with a story that teaches about humility and respect. This was one of six stories I learned over the past year in one of the classes offered through the Intergenerational Secwepemctsín Fluency Model. This is the language revitalization research project in which I am currently collaborating with Eastern and Northern communities. The story was taught in Level 1 Eastern Secwepemctsín class, so it is a shorter version for beginners. I am grateful to Elders Lucy Williams and Flora Sampson for teaching me this story.

R Mégce (The Moon)

Nek̓wu7eses r mégce swinúmtc-ekwe.
Once upon a time, it was said that The Moon was beautiful.

M cwesétes-ekwe ne s7istk, m-yístes t̓ri7 we7 t̓henes.
During the winter months, they travelled about and camped anywhere.

M-cetcnémes m- k̓ulct.s r se7é7es ell stsmet.s t̓e cyísteṅs.
He went ahead and made camp for his wife and children.

R se7é7es skwest.s Wala.
His wife's name was Wala.

Sewes r sxelwes, "T̓ he7e me7 k̓ últcwes re7 stsmelt t̓e cyísteṅ?"
She asked her husband, "Where are you going to make camps for the children?"

Gyep-ekwe r Mégce, m-tsútes, "Yíst-ce nen skwetús."
The Moon got mad, he shouted, "Camp on my face!"

Necwetés r sxélwes, m-llgwílcwes ne skwetúst.s r sxélwes.
She believed her husband and jumped on his face.

Pyin me7 wiktc r Wala ṫe tskwestés r llkepépye7s ell lepéls ne mégce.
Now when you look at The Moon, you see Wala holding her pot and
shovel on the moon.

Conclusions

Strong relationships are grounded in trust and built by getting to know
each other. This structured reflection was an effort to develop a deeper
understanding of Secwépemc culture, so I can build new respectful relationships and strengthen existing ones. Through learning Secwepemctsín,
I have learned about Secwépemc belief systems, values, laws, protocols,
decision-making practices, relationship building (with each other, the animals, the land, and all things on it), the history of their land and their
people, their humanity.

While I could highlight numerous learnings, the most salient one for
me is the symbiotic nature of the Secwépemc language and their culture.
As examined throughout this paper, Secwepemctsín reflects, encodes, and
reveals important values that form part of the Secwépemc world view and
culture; these include strong connections with the land, kinship and relational accountability and reciprocity, humility, and respect. Awareness
of these symbiotic relationships allowed me to see more clearly why the
colonial policy of banning language, which was rigorously implemented
in residential schools, was an attack on Indigenous peoples. It was a
clear, intentional, and systematic effort to eradicate Indigenous cultures,
Indigenous identities. For the Secwépemc and other Indigenous groups,
this devastating loss of their language was a loss of their world, their culture,
their identity. Engaging in collaboration with the Secwépemc and learning
Secwepemctsín has helped me understand the meaning and tragic dimen-
sion of this loss. This preparation is essential to becoming an effective ally.

A language facilitates the transmission of ideas, values, knowledge,
but most importantly, emotions. Our emotions are deeply encoded in our
mother tongue. My heart vibrates at the rhythm of my tongue when I roll
my r's, *rrrrrrr* in Spanish, my mother tongue. I relish in the unconstrained
utterance of my Spanish vowels. I feel liberated and at ease when I speak
it. It is my language, my mother tongue. It allows me to laugh my heart out
like no other language I speak; it allows me to fully enjoy the subtleties of
humour; jokes get lost in translation.

When I think of this, I also think about the Secwépemc and what they
have lost by not being able to speak their language, the language of their

ancestors, the language of their heart. It is only in one's mother tongue that one can express the deepest emotions. As eloquently expressed in a quote attributed to Nelson Mandela, "If you talk to a man in a language he understands, that goes to his head. If you talk to him in his own language, that goes to his heart" (Peace Corps, 1996, p. vi). To connect to their ancestors, the Secwépemc and all other Indigenous peoples should be able to speak their language.

Land, identity, law, culture, and language are intertwined in Secwépemc world views. As such, any attempt to decolonize teaching and research praxis and to honour Secwépemc people should include Secwepemctsín. Secwepemctsín revitalization is an act of decolonization and speaking Secwepemctsín is an act of insurgence and resurgence. Learning a language, just like truly getting to know people and building relationships and trust, takes time, dedication, and persistence. As I continue it with humility, I need to learn to embrace vulnerability and uncertainty. I need to learn to trust that things will make sense at some point. Knowing this will give me the strength to follow an unknown and uncertain path.

References

Arango, P. M., & Uribe, T. S. (n.d.). *Marinilla reseña histórica.* https://marinillaantioquia .micolombiadigital.gov.co/sites/marinillaantioquia/content/files/000002/74_ resena-historica.pdf

Billy, J. (2009). *Back from the brink: Decolonizing through the restoration of Secwépemc language, culture, and identity* [Unpublished doctoral thesis]. Simon Fraser University.

Chiblow, S., & Meighan, P. (2022). Language is land, land is language: The importance of Indigenous languages. *Human Geography*, 15(2), 206–210. https://doi. org/10.1177/19427786211022899

Colombia's Constitution of 1991 with Amendments through 2015. (2015). Oxford University Press, Inc. https://www.constituteproject.org/constitution/Colombia_2015.pdf? lang=en

Crystal, D. (2010). *The Cambridge encyclopedia of language* (3rd ed.). Cambridge University Press.

Davis, W. (2009). *The wayfinders: Why ancient wisdom matters in the modern world.* House of Anansi Press.

El Santuario, Antioquia: Capital agrícola de Antioquia. (n.d.). Oriente Antioqueño. https://orienteantioqueno.com/el-santuario/

Gottfriedson, G., Airini, & Matthew, T. (2022). *The Secwépemc Nation research ethics guidelines.* Thompson Rivers University. https://www.tru.ca/__shared/assets/ secwepemc-nation-research-ethics-guidelines55048.pdf

Ignace, M. (2022). *Making the most of teaching and learning* [Keynote address]. TRU Teaching Practices Colloquium, Thompson Rivers University, Kamloops, BC, Canada.

Ignace, M., & Ignace, R. (2017). *Secwépemc people, land, and laws: Yerí7 re Stsq'ey's-kucw.* McGill-Queen's University Press.

López Lozano, C. (1968). *Rionegro: Narraciones sobre su historia.* Editorial Granamérica.

Peace Corps. (1996). *At home in the world: the Peace Corps story.* https://babel. hathitrust.org/cgi/pt?id=uc1.b4155929&seq=36

Risager, K. (2006). *Language and culture. Global flows and local complexity.* Clevedon: Multilingual Matters, pp. 185–199.

Sistema Nacional de Información Cultural. (n.d.). Arqueología-Antioquia. https:// www.sinic.gov.co/SINIC/ColombiaCultural/ColCulturalBusca.aspx?AREID=3 &SECID=8&IdDep=05&COLTEM=211

Truth and Reconciliation Commission of Canada. (2015). *Honouring the truth, reconciling for the future: summary of the final report of the Truth and Reconciliation Commission of Canada.* https://ehprnh2mwo3.exactdn.com/wp-content/uploads/ 2021/01/Executive_Summary_English_Web.pdf

Turner, N. J., Ignace, M., & Ignace, R. (2000). Traditional ecological knowledge and wisdom of Aboriginal Peoples in British Columbia. *Ecological Applications,* 10(5), 1275–1287.

HEALTH CALLS
TO ACTION

The Truth and Reconciliation Commission (2015, pp. 2–3) includes seven Calls to Action in relation to health. Issues named as priorities for change in relation to health by the Calls to Action:

18. We call upon the federal, provincial, territorial, and Aboriginal governments to acknowledge that the current state of Aboriginal health in Canada is a direct result of previous Canadian government policies, including residential schools, and to recognize and implement the health-care rights of Aboriginal people as identified in international law, constitutional law, and under the Treaties.

19. We call upon the federal government, in consultation with Aboriginal peoples, to establish measurable goals to identify and close the gaps in health outcomes between Aboriginal and non-Aboriginal communities, and to publish annual progress reports and assess long-term trends. Such efforts would focus on indicators such as: infant mortality, maternal health, suicide, mental health, addictions, life expectancy, birth rates, infant and child health issues, chronic diseases, illness and injury incidence, and the availability of appropriate health services.

20. In order to address the jurisdictional disputes concerning Aboriginal people who do not reside on reserves, we call

upon the federal government to recognize, respect, and address the distinct health needs of the Métis, Inuit, and off-reserve Aboriginal peoples.

21. We call upon the federal government to provide sustainable funding for existing and new Aboriginal healing centres to address the physical, mental, emotional, and spiritual harms caused by residential schools, and to ensure that the funding of healing centres in Nunavut and the Northwest Territories is a priority.

22. We call upon those who can effect change within the Canadian health-care system to recognize the value of Aboriginal healing practices and use them in the treatment of Aboriginal patients in collaboration with Aboriginal healers and Elders where requested by Aboriginal patients.

23. We call upon all levels of government to:
     i.   Increase the number of Aboriginal professionals working in the health-care field.
     ii. Ensure the retention of Aboriginal health-care providers in Aboriginal communities.
     iii. Provide cultural competency training for all health-care professionals.

24. We call upon medical and nursing schools in Canada to require all students to take a course dealing Aboriginal health issues, including the history and legacy of residential schools, the *United Nations Declaration on the Rights of Indigenous Peoples*, Treaties, and Aboriginal rights, and Indigenous teachings and practices. This will require skills-based training in intercultural competency, conflict resolution, human rights, and anti-racism.

References

Truth and Reconciliation Commission of Canada. (2015). Calls to Action. Winnipeg, Manitoba.   https://ehprnh2mwo3.exactdn.com/wp-content/uploads/2021/01/Calls_to_Action_English2.pdf

lessons

Garry Gottfriedson

pungent scent
fills his catholic room
silent moon weeps

wild sweat thickens air
the window is closed
his barbed face burning

the child beneath him
learning to die in moments like this
was never taught these things in catechism

dropping to his knees
for any savior was a lesson
never to be forgotten

and knowing god's son
did not die for reason
quickly dried bloodshot eyes

irrationally he thinks
these walls were built for him
making anything bleed

flogging turns him on
for redemption
but doesn't bend god's ear

kindness does
children die
knowing this

still scars are forever
reminders
they will be seen in stark daylight

Grave Concerns

Rod McCormick

Abstract

This chapter explores the idea that reconciliation is seen by many Indigenous peoples in Canada as "re-conceal-iation." The author suggests that Canada has been able to evade acceptance of, and to further conceal and re-conceal, its awful history with Indigenous peoples under the auspices of reconciliation through various stalling tactics. These stalling tactics consist of governmental commissions and inquiries that make recommendations, calls to action, and calls to justice that are largely unrealized. The author proposes that, going forward, reconciliation be conducted with compassion, respect, contrition, and restitution.

It may seem strange to title this short chapter in a book discussing reconciliation as "Grave Concerns"; however, I use the term "grave" in a purposeful manner. As my partner and children are members of Tk'emlúps te Secwépemc, and I live in their community, I experienced firsthand the impact of the announcement of the 215 children's graves in the grounds of the former residential school. I can clearly see the residential school from the windows of my house and can glimpse the fields in which at least 215 children have been buried in shallow, unmarked graves. This attempt to conceal the bodies is in some ways symbolic of the numerous attempts by Canada to deal with what Deputy Superintendent of Indian Affairs Duncan Campbell Scott referred to as the need to get rid of the "Indian problem" (as cited in *"Until There Is Not a Single Indian in Canada,"* 2020).

FIGURE 2.1. Grave concerns; *left to right*: Fred Schaub, Rod McCormick, Hilda Green, and Natalie Clark.
Source: Victoria Handford.

As I write this there is an all-day memorial in the residential school grounds at Tk'emlúps to mark the one-year anniversary of the announcement of the uncovered children's graves. Many government leaders are in attendance, including the Governor General and the prime minister. Her Excellency, Mary Simon, the first Indigenous Governor General in the history of Canada, said that the time for "I didn't know" is over. Since the Tk'emlúps announcement last year, approximately 20 former residential schools have located unmarked graves, which now number in the thousands. Yet most Canadians are still saying "I didn't know."

I sometimes refer to "reconciliation," sarcastically, as "Re-conceal-iation" (McCormick, 2020). I believe that Canada has been able to evade acceptance of, and to further conceal and re-conceal, its awful history with Indigenous peoples under the auspices of reconciliation through stalling tactics. In modern times this includes the launching of the Royal Commission on Aboriginal Peoples (it lasted six years), the Truth and Reconciliation Commission (it lasted six years), the National Inquiry into Missing and Murdered Indigenous Women and Girls (MMIWG; it lasted three years) (see MMIWG, 2019; Royal Commission on Aboriginal Peoples, 1993; Truth and Reconciliation Commission of Canada, 2015). By studying and re-studying the problem, different federal governments effectively concealed and evaded addressing the age-old "Indian problem" for yet another 15 years. The recent confirmation that thousands of bodies of Indigenous children were buried without their graves being marked has made such government strategies gravely inappropriate; the horrific treatment of Indigenous children in these schools can no longer be concealed. Increasing numbers of bodies are being located and will slowly be removed from the ground. Conjecture about these atrocities can no longer be an intellectual exercise. The bodies of those children will be respectfully repatriated and buried. The burden of this responsibility unfortunately falls on the shoulders of Indigenous peoples.

My children's *kye7e* (grandmother) attended the Kamloops Indian Residential School from the age of 5 to 18. That is an entire childhood. Despite this, she resolutely remained a Catholic until her death. The Catholic Church remains the only institution which did not pay their small portion of the Indian Residential Schools Settlement Agreement even though they operated 70 percent of the schools (Canada et al., 2006). Other Churches named in the settlement agreement demonstrated good faith in making restitution, in some cases by selling off church land (Galloway & Fine, 2016). As a former Catholic, I remember that part of the Catholic sacrament of reconciliation (also known as confession or penance) is "restitution." In Fr. John Hardon's *Modern Catholic Dictionary*, we learn that restitution means returning to its rightful owner whatever has been unjustly taken from that person (as cited in Catholic Culture, n.d.). No sin can be pardoned without sincere contrition and a firm purpose of amendment (Slater, 1908). The Catholic Church has not been following its own teachings when it comes to Indigenous peoples. In many ways this can be said of other religions as well.

The data on the mistreatment of Indigenous peoples are irrefutable. Just last week an announcement was made that Indigenous women now account for half of the female population in federal penitentiaries, a situation Canada's prison ombudsman calls "shocking and shameful" (Polson, 2022). Just over a year ago, British Columbia (BC) released the results of its *In Plain Sight* (Turpel-Lafond, 2020) report. The report found that most Indigenous people in BC have encountered racism and discrimination within our health care system, whether as a patient or a health care worker. Indigenous respondents described experiencing stereotyping, unacceptable personal interactions, and poorer quality of care; they also noted that they do not feel safe when accessing health care services and interacting with health providers (Turpel-Lafond, 2020). COVID has made the health care challenges of Indigenous peoples disproportionally worse. Opioid overdoses among Indigenous peoples were five to eight times higher for Indigenous peoples pre-COVID (Lavalley et al., 2018). Since COVID those rates have almost doubled. This does not just have to do with illegal opiates; Statistics Canada found that in 2018 physicians prescribed Indigenous people opiates twice as often as non-Indigenous patients (Carriere et al., 2022; Statistics Canada, 2019).

Duncan Campbell Scott, who oversaw the Indian residential school system for Aboriginal children, meant to get rid of the Indians through any means necessary. That mission, it seems, has never been abandoned. In many ways his goal to "get rid of the Indian problem" became emblematic of the federal and provincial government's treatment of Indigenous peoples. A partial list of the means by which this was carried out would include forced sterilization; forced relocation to reserves with unsafe, unhealthy, crowded housing; the use of blankets infected with the smallpox virus; the residential schools, the ongoing child welfare seizure of Indigenous children, the disproportionate imprisonment of Indigenous people in the penal system, malnutrition experiments with Indigenous children, the removal of food sources such as bison; ignoring the tuberculosis risks in residential schools; and much, much more (Appel, 2021; APTN, 2020; Clark, 2019; Gill, 2015; Mercer, 2019; Mosby, 2013; Stote, 2015; Truth and Reconciliation, 2015; Waiser, 2021; White, 2022).

Another recent development about which I have grave concerns is the revision of the Medical Assistance in Dying (MAiD) law (2021). Two years ago, I testified to Senate on the first revision, which proposed allowing those with a mental illness to access MAiD. Canadian physicians have asked me to respond to the most recent revision, which will also extend MAiD to minors and those with disabilities. When Indigenous adults and children are already overrepresented at every stage of the health system, it seems ironic to provide yet another path to death. As a result of the multitude of ways Canada has used to eliminate Indigenous peoples and culture, we are overrepresented at every stage of the health care system including that of premature deaths. This may all seem overly dramatic, but do we really need another path to death? My cynicism is partly based on decades of working with Indigenous youth to help them attain and maintain a good and healthy life. Granted, there are those suffering from irremediable physical illnesses that may under some circumstances benefit from MAiD, but those are extreme exceptions.

I have worked with many Indigenous youth in emotional pain who recovered from being suicidal. The common reflection they had was one of relief that they did not choose a permanent solution to what proved to be a temporary problem. Getting proper and timely help is the key to survival. Unfortunately, that help is not easy to come by. Many barriers keep people from obtaining that help. Among the obstacles are a lack of accurate diagnosis and corresponding treatment; a racist health care system; a mistrust of the health care system who do not always have our "best interest" in mind; jurisdictional ambiguity; the abdication of responsibility by various governments. The key factor is the remoteness and lack of access to necessary and life-saving resources of many of our communities (Allan & Smylie, 2015; Richmond & Cook, 2016; Vogel, 2015). Living on reserve and/or in a remote location often means that health services are provided by nurses or nurse practitioners who are overworked and ill-prepared to provide the required range of services. Because of COVID we have seen an increase in domestic violence, suicide, and drug overdoses (Mashford-Pringle et al., 2021).

The message that MAiD presents to those who are suffering is that when the suffering becomes more than they can tolerate, they can have their lives ended by medical professionals. This message undermines the whole concept of suicide prevention. As another witness once said, medical assistance in living is preferable to medical assistance in dying. As an Indigenous academic and mental health professional I am perplexed as to why mental health resources only flow freely to Indigenous communities when they declare a state of emergency due to an extreme number of suicides or drug overdoses. Those same resources are not available for prevention purposes. It is hard not to be cynical when governments refuse to move the continuum of care upstream from postvention to prevention. Trudo Lemmens, the Scholl Chair in Health Law and Policy at the University of Toronto, told *The Hill Times* that the government has "prioritized this ending of life on the basis of an abstract notion of autonomy, without recognizing the social context" (Benson, 2022).

The pattern I am seeing in the introduction of this legislation is that of an abdication of responsibility by the government of Canada and, by extension, the citizens of Canada. Instead of making every effort to provide the range of mental health services needed by Indigenous and non-Indigenous youth to overcome their pain, we are instead imposing upon them the responsibility to decide if they must choose a permanent solution to what could easily be a temporary problem.

That is where mainstream Canadian cultural values fail us all. The emphasis on individual rights and individual freedom is not balanced with the need for collective responsibility. The lack of this collective responsibility has become all too evident by means of the denial and lack of action regarding the environment and our inevitable experience of global warming and environmental disasters.

Indigenous peoples long ago recognized our interdependence with the earth and all of creation, be it two-legged or four-legged. The Western individualistic value of the right to be free of collective responsibility to the land has meant that Indigenous peoples, as the original guardians of the land, needed to be removed (buried) so that the valuable minerals and trees and so on could be dug up instead. Neither the exploitation of the environment nor the exploitation of this country's Indigenous peoples can be reconciled, nor can they remain concealed or re-concealed through denial or endless studies. Today, I also listened to Prime Minister Justin Trudeau say, "We will continue to remember the children who never returned," and that "It is on all of us to remember them and to honour them."

Tk'emlúps and the Secwépemc peoples have a name for the buried children; it is Le Estcwicwèẏ (The Missing). This naming was a conscious decision made by the Tk'emlúps knowledge keepers not to use a number such as 215 because children who attended the schools were given numbers and referred to by their numbers and not their names. Although it might seem easier to leave those children buried in shallow graves across Canada, most Indigenous people feel that we must find them and return them to their homes and families. There is no roadmap for doing this, but it is being done with compassion and respect.

Similarly, reconciliation in Canada has no roadmap. Up until now it has been easier for Canadians to conceal and to bury this shameful history. Not having known this history is not a reason for continuing to conceal it. Because of the international notoriety associated with Le Estcwicwèẏ, three Indigenous Catholic communities in Canada were visited by the pope in 2022, so he would have the opportunity to apologize to Indigenous peoples for the shameful history of the church. In keeping with the Catholic sacrament of reconciliation, the hope was the apology would constitute acceptance of responsibility by the church. As would be keeping with reconciliation, this would have been done with compassion, respect, contrition, and restitution. Someday, this may occur with both the church and with Canadians. Canadians feel compelled to do this.

References

Allan, B., & Smylie, J. (2015). *First Peoples, second class treatment: The role of racism in the health and well-being of Indigenous peoples in Canada*. The Wellesley Institute.

Appel, J. (2021, July 18). Researchers say that TB at residential schools was no accident. *CTV News*. https://www.ctvnews.ca/canada/researchers-say-that-tb-at-residential-schools-was-no-accident-1.5513755

APTN National News. (2020, May 5). Child welfare system continuing assimilation begun by Indian Residential Schools: TRC. *APTN News*. https://www.aptnnews.ca/national-news/child-welfare-system-continuing-assimilation-begun-indian-residential-schools-trc/

Benson, S. (2022, August 22). 'These are real people': medical ethicist urges Parliamentarians to dig deeper on inappropriate MAID applications. *The Hill Times*. https://www.hilltimes.com/story/2022/08/22/these-are-real-people-medical-ethicist-urges-parliamentarians-to-dig-deeper-on-inappropriate-maid-applications/231233/

Canada, Plaintiffs, The Assembly of First Nations and Inuit Representatives, The General Synod of the Anglican Church of Canada, The Presbyterian Church of Canada, & The United Church of Canada and Roman Catholic Entities. (2006, May 8). *Indian Residential Schools Settlement Agreement*. https://www.residentialschoolsettlement.ca/settlement.html

Carriere, G., Garner, R., & Sanmartin, C. (2022, January 19). *Significant factors associated with problematic use of opioid pain relief medications among the household population, Canada, 2018*. Statistics Canada. https://www.doi.org/10.25318/82-003-x202101200002-eng

Catholic Culture. (n.d.). *Catholic Dictionary: RESTITUTION*. https://www.catholicculture.org/culture/library/dictionary/index.cfm?id=36075

Clark, S. (2019). *Overrepresentation of Indigenous people in the Canadian criminal justice system: Causes and responses*. Department of Justice Canada. https://www.justice.gc.ca/eng/rp-pr/jr/oip-cjs/oip-cjs-en.pdf

Deroy, S., & Schütze, H. (2019, May 15). Factors supporting retention of aboriginal health and wellbeing staff in Aboriginal health services: A comprehensive review of the literature. *International Journal of Equity Health*, 18(1), 70. https://doi.org/10.1186/s12939-019-0968-4

Galloway, G., & Fine, S. (2016, April 27). Other churches escape residential school settlement obligations in wake of Catholic deal. *The Globe and Mail*. https://

www.theglobeandmail.com/news/politics/churches-escape-residential-school-settlement-obligations-in-wake-of-catholic-deal/article29767422/

Gill, J. (2017, April 29). 'Extirpate this execrable race': The dark history of Jeffery Amherst. *CBC News*. https://www.cbc.ca/news/canada/prince-edward-island/jeffery-amherst-history-complex-1.4089019

Lavalley, J., Kastor, S., Valleriani, J., & McNeil, R. (2018). Reconciliation and Canada's overdose crisis: responding to the needs of Indigenous peoples. *Canadian Medical Association Journal*, 190(50), E1466–E1467. https://doi.org/10.1503/cmaj.181093

Mashford-Pringle, A., Skura, C., Stutz, S., & Yohathasan, T. (2021, February). *What we heard: Indigenous peoples and COVID-19: Supplementary report for the Chief Public Health Officer of Canada's report on the state of public health in Canada*. Public Health Agency of Canada. https://www.canada.ca/content/dam/phac-aspc/documents/corporate/publications/chief-public-health-officer-reports-state-public-health-canada/from-risk-resilience-equity-approach-covid-19/indigenous-peoples-covid-19-report/cpho-wwh-report-en.pdf

Mercer, G. (2019, March 8). 'Beggars in our own land': Canada's first nation housing crisis. *The Guardian*. https://www.theguardian.com/cities/2019/mar/08/beggars-in-our-own-land-canadas-first-nation-housing-crisis

Mosby, I. (2013). Administering colonial science: Nutrition research and human biomedical experimentation in Aboriginal communities and residential schools, 1942–1952. *Histoire Sociale/Social History*, 46(91), 145–172.

The National Inquiry into Missing and Murdered Indigenous Women and Girls [MMIWG]. (2019, May 29). *Reclaiming Power and Place: The Final Report of the National Inquiry into Missing and Murdered Indigenous Women and Girls*. www.mmiwg-ffada.ca/final-report

Polson, M. (2022, May 6). *Investigator calls Canada's prison state of affairs 'shocking and shameful'.* The Raven. https://www.theraven.fm/news1/raven-country-news/correctional-investigator-calls-canadas-prison-state-of-affairs-shocking-and-shameful/

Richmond, C. A. M., & Cook, C. (2016). Creating conditions for Canadian aboriginal health equity: the promise of healthy public policy. *Public Health Rev* 37(2). https://doi.org/10.1186/s40985-016-0016-5

Slater, T. (1908). Restitution: From the *Catholic Encyclopedia*. Mary Foundation at Catholic City. https://www.catholicity.com/encyclopedia/r/restitution.html#:~:text=From%20the%20Catholic%20Encyclopedia%20Restitution%20has%20a%20special,an%20injury%20that%20has%20been%20done%20to%20another

Statistics Canada. (2019). *Pain relief medication containing opioids, 2018*. https://www150.statcan.gc.ca/n1/pub/82-625-x/2019001/article/00008-eng.htm

Stote, K. (2015). *An act of genocide: Colonialism and the sterilization of aboriginal women*. Fernwood Publishing.

Truth and Reconciliation Commission of Canada. (2015). *Canada's residential schools: Reconciliation* (Vol. 6). McGill-Queen's University Press.

Turpel-Lafond, M. (2020). *In plain sight: Addressing Indigenous-specific racism and discrimination in BC health care.* British Columbia. https://engage.gov.bc.ca/app/uploads/sites/613/2020/11/In-Plain-Sight-Summary-Report.pdf

"Until There Is Not a Single Indian in Canada." (2020, July 28). Facing History & Ourselves Canada. https://www.facinghistory.org/en-ca/resource-library/until-there-is-not-single-indian-canada

Vogel, L. (2015, January 6). *Broken trust drives native health disparities.* CMAJ News. https://www.cmaj.ca/content/cmaj/187/1/E9.full.pdf

Waiser, B. (2021, September 5). Whither the bison: What happened to the prairies' once mighty herds? *CBC News.* https://www.cbc.ca/news/canada/saskatchewan/waiser-history-whither-the-bison-1.6154180

White, P. (2022, May 5). 'Shocking and shameful': For the first time, Indigenous women make up half the female population in Canada's federal prisons. *The Globe and Mail.* https://www.theglobeandmail.com/canada/article-half-of-all-women-inmates-are-indigenous/

A Walk Together

Bernita Wienhold-Leahy

She hears strange beeping, clicking, and far-off cries. Disinfectant hits her nostrils and filters into her senses. The feeling of the hard bed rouses her into consciousness; without opening her eyes, she knows that she is back in the hospital. She must have overdosed again. She can sense another person in the room. She falls back into a listless existence.

A cart bangs against the bed; the nurse needs to take her vitals; she knows the drill. Arm extended, mouth open, she follows procedure. She knows it doesn't help to complain; they just like her even less. They bring her a plate of what she always calls "gruel." She tries to swallow a mouthful, but the taste is indescribable. She adds the sugar they brought for her tea, which arrived cold. It makes it slightly better. She can swallow a couple more mouthfuls. She needs to eat to pretend she is well enough to get out of here. She knows the drill.

The girl next to her plays with her breakfast in obvious distaste. Maybe she doesn't know the sugar trick. Maybe this is her first time here. A form beside her bed starts to move; it is an old woman with deep wrinkles and a kind face; she must be the girl's grandmother. She speaks to the girl in a caring, soothing voice in an unrecognizable language. Her voice sings like the beat of a drum. It is comforting, yet has a force to it. Soon the old woman leaves.

The two girls eye each other, but silence ensues. No words are exchanged over mystery dinners of mashed potatoes, some kind of meat product, and overcooked peas and carrots. There isn't anything to say. Nurses return

FIGURE 2.2. Building understanding with Bernita Wienhold-Leahy (*left*) and Natalie Clark (*right*).
Source: Victoria Handford.

with rumbling carts for more vitals. Arms extended, mouths open, they know the drill.

Crying disturbs the night. The girl beside her whimpers; dreams disturb her sleep. The girl's crying annoys her, and she tries to ignore it without success. What should she do? Call the nurses? The nurses wouldn't do anything anyway. They are too overworked to care about a lousy dream. They might even make it worse. She crosses the room to the girl, who, at this point, is crying in distress. This is the first time she has had a good look at the girl. Her long, dark hair lies softly against the pillow, and her light brown face is distorted in grief or fear; it is hard to know which.

She speaks to the girl in a quiet, soothing voice, like she heard her grandmother do earlier. She thinks maybe her soft, gentle voice will rouse her out of her nightmare. The girl's eyes fly open in fear, eyes darting around the room before resting on her. A look of confusion sets in. What does *she* want? Why is *she* here? The girl says her first words to her: "Go away. Leave me alone."

Sunlight filters through the dusty windows; nurses return for the morning ritual. Arms out, mouths open, more gruel, the girls know the drill. They peer at each other, this time in curiosity.

"My name is Judy. Are you okay? You had a pretty bad dream last night."

"My name is Kateri, and I have lots of bad dreams. The doctors say I have post-traumatic stress disorder. Thanks for waking me. People don't usually care about me."

Judy understands, "Ya, me too. I get brought here whenever my mom needs a break from me. She hates me."

Beeps, clatter, and the clanking of carts rolling down hallways continue. Both girls try to dwindle the time away. They complain to each other about the horrible food; they wonder how eating hospital food could have ever helped anyone become healthy. Kateri shares her knowledge of eating from the land. Both girls crave natural, nutritious food. Doctors visit; nurses take vitals. Boredom sets in while they stare out the window to the clear, blue sky. In silence, both dream about being outdoors and free from their confinement.

Suddenly, Kateri says, "Let's get out of here!" With that, she gets up and starts getting dressed. Bewildered, Judy also begins putting on her clothes. Excitement stirs in the girls. Escaping the hospital is remarkably easy for the duo. Before they know it, they are on the street, in a full run, increasing their distance from the hospital. When they reach the city park, they sit down by a riverbank, exhausted.

Watching the water flow by, they sit in silence. Mesmerized, neither wants to break the quiet as they watch the ducks, swans, and geese swoop down and settle on the river. A gentle breeze brings a freshness and lightness to the air. The girls relax in the moment, their thoughts floating away with the clouds in the sky. Moments became hours; the whisper of the wind and water lapping against the shores brings a natural calmness. Time floats by.

"Soul wound," Kateri says quietly, almost in a whisper. "That is what Elder Claire told me yesterday. She said I have a soul wound." Neither speak; the words "soul wound" settle on their minds.

"Did Elder Claire tell you how to cure your soul wound?" asks Judy.

"She said for me to connect with my community as my own family can't help me anymore. She also told me to find my strengths." Kateri's words linger in the silence. An eagle swoops down and alights atop a towering spruce; frogs croak in the distance; a salmon flicks its tail.

"Wow, it's beautiful here. Really beautiful. I've been to this park a zillion times, but I never realized how peaceful it can be," voices Judy.

"Elder Claire says all creatures on this earth have a role to play; some provide us with food while some teach us lessons. We thank the Creator for providing us with our rich environment. We need to care for all the creatures on this earth," states Kateri in response.

Until this moment, Judy never appreciated the beauty of nature nor its creatures. She always seemed to be too caught up in her own problems to notice. "I think it took strength and courage to run away from the hospital.

I wouldn't have done that on my own, and I am glad you took me with you. Perhaps these are your strengths Elder Claire spoke of."

"Hmmm. Maybe. Thank you for waking me up from my nightmare. Even though I was a stranger, you helped me. You were very gentle and kind. Perhaps these are your strengths." Once again, the girls sit in stillness.

"How can we learn more from Elder Claire?" queries Judy.

"Let's go find her," states Kateri with excitement. "I think there is much to learn from her."

The eagle departs its perch and soars off into the distance.

Health Care Practices

Bernita Wienhold-Leahy

Abstract

Traditional Indigenous practices of health care focus on a holistic practice of care. Prior to colonization, Indigenous people lived in harmony with the land, and they practiced a community wellness approach based on preventative care. The children were the centre of the community, and they grew up with strong, healthy attachments. Since colonization, the physical and mental health of Indigenous people has deteriorated due to introduced diseases, changes in diet, being confined to reserve lands, loss of cultural practices, and the removal of children from their families. Truth and Reconciliation Calls to Action on health care state that Indigenous wellness practices and more Indigenous health care practitioners need to be integrated into the health care system. Traditional Indigenous practices grounded in a strengths-based approach can be a foundation of health and wellness for Indigenous and non-Indigenous people in Canada.

Yucwmentsut (translated as "Health—Look after yourself").
Secwépemc Health Caucus, 2022

My personal experience with health care practices in Canada have made me aware that the health care system is overwhelmed, and practitioners are often overworked, desensitized, and lack compassion. Prescription drugs are the go-to for health care practitioners. I believe, especially with a pandemic as a backdrop to this research, that our health care system needs transformation, including the use of alternative principles and practices of care. What our health care requires is more understanding of the individual needs of patients. This includes a more holistic vision of health care practices instead of a dependence on pharmaceuticals. Holistic care would provide a focus on the physical, mental, and spiritual needs of patients. Specifically, for Indigenous people in Canada, health care practitioners require understanding based on ancient knowledge and wisdom of Indigenous cultural practices.

While more Indigenous people are being trained in health care, the medical field predominantly employs non-Indigenous staff who are not trained in Indigenous practices. As a result, Indigenous people often receive medical interventions that are not in line with their traditional practices. Ninety-four Calls to Action (Truth and Reconciliation Commission of Canada [TRC], 2015) have been developed to create an ongoing dialogue between First Nations, Métis, Inuit, survivors of the residential schools and their families, the public, and the government to draw attention to past injustices and develop standards to foster reconciliation and healing: "By incorporating Indigenous perspectives, values, laws and protocols, we are creating something new—we are striving to decolonize the archive and be built on principles of respect, honesty, wisdom, courage, humility, love, and truth" (National Centre for Truth and Reconciliation, 2022, para. 7).

In this chapter, I first review the Calls to Action that address health care, followed by a short description of pre-colonial Indigenous and health care practices and discuss the harms created by government policies and the Indian residential schools. I also draw attention to the injustices that prevail in many institutions in Canada, with a focus on the medical system. I explore Indigenous wellness practices, suggest the need for a more holistic view of health care, and highlight existing programs that address building resilience and wellness for Indigenous youth.

The Truth and Reconciliation Calls to Action

The Truth and Reconciliation Calls to Action are guidelines developed to improve conditions and make concrete changes to many aspects of society, including the health care system (TRC, 2015). Call to Action 18 states that the government needs to acknowledge that the current state (negative) of Aboriginal health is a direct result of government policies and interventions in the lives of the people. The government needs to acknowledge past harms and implement policies to recognize the rights of Aboriginal people.

Call to Action 22 states a need to recognize and integrate Aboriginal healing practices in the treatment of Aboriginal clients and patients with the help of traditional healers and Elders (TRC, 2015). This requires an increase in traditional Aboriginal healers in the medical field by increasing Indigenous professionals in the health care system. More awareness and cultural competency on traditional health practices is required for all health care professionals.

Call to Action 24 states a need to teach Indigenous practices to medical practitioners, including through courses to discuss past government policies and to teach "skills-based training in intercultural competency, conflict resolution, human rights, and anti-racism" (TRC, 2015, p. 3).

In addition, Call to Action 21 demands funding for healing centres based on traditional practices to address the "physical, mental, emotional, and spiritual harms caused by residential schools" (p. 3). Call to Action 66 asks that funding must also be created for programming for Indigenous youth to learn more about traditional practices.

Clearly, much work is required to increase awareness of past injustices to Indigenous peoples in Canada, to learn about traditional Indigenous health practices, to integrate Indigenous health practices into health care training, and to provide funding for programs and treatment centres based on traditional Indigenous practices.

Pre-Colonial Lives of Indigenous People

> Our Creation story informs us that Old One and Coyote created the world we now inhabit. They provided instructions of how we must live and responsibilities we must uphold so we would always live in harmony and balance with Mother Earth. (Billy, 2009, p. 2)

Prior to the arrival of Europeans, the Indigenous peoples of the interior of British Columbia lived in synchrony with each other and their environment (First Nations Health Authority [FNHA], 2022). They hunted wild game, fished in nearby rivers and streams, and collected fruit and vegetables off the land. They lived in harmony with Mother Earth (Turner, 2017). They had local knowledge of their ecosystem and observed environmental practices (Coffey et al., 1990). They were physically strong, mentally and emotionally well, and had vital spiritual beliefs. There was a strong sense of community and harmony with the animals and their environment (First Nations Health Council [FNHC], 2011). Traditional healing was centred on a strengths-based approach, which emphasized the strengths of the individual, family, or community (Brave Heart et al., 2012). Indigenous people practised spiritual healing with the use of traditional plants and herbs. The focus was on individual and community wellness based on a preventive care approach (FNHA, 2022). Ceremonies, prayers, songs, and dances facilitated healing, a sense of belonging, and a link to the history of the people (Coffey et al., 1990).

Through traditional ceremonies, participants developed healthy attachments. For example, a naming ceremony among Secwépemc people provided members of the community with a sense of belonging (Billy, 2009). New children born into the community were welcomed in ceremony, and the community affirmed their commitment to helping raise the child. In addition, sweat lodge ceremonies were used for physical and spiritual cleansing (Billy, 2009). Additionally, when anyone was feeling troubled, they would go to the water to cleanse their mind. A vision quest was another ceremony where one would be in a meditative state by fasting and being in seclusion in nature (McCormick & Amundson, 1997). Visions or dreams became a pathway to healing or to experience a new sense of awareness and identity.

The focus on individual and community wellness included raising children and caring for each other as a community (FNHA, 2022). Among the Secwépemc people, the family formed the circle around the children, and the whole family cared for the children (Billy, 2009). If parents could no longer take care of their family, other members such as aunts, uncles, or grandparents stepped in and helped raise the children (Ignace & Ignace, 2017). The older children also helped the younger children. The land was the school (Billy, 2009). "Children were rarely scolded, and the purpose of education was to empower children" (Billy, 2009, p. 44). Child rearing centred on a sense of belonging and opportunities for mastery, encouraging independence; generosity was extolled as a virtue. Learning was purposeful and meaningful. Parental practices were focused on building upon strengths (Billy, 2009).

The Indigenous Elders recognized the importance of passing on their traditional ways to the children to preserve their way of life (Jules, 1996). Educational principles among the Secwépemc people included observation and imitation (Haig-Brown, 1988; Jules, 1996). The children learned the value of sharing and respect to family and of food and the natural world (Billy, 2009). Other qualities were cooperation, perseverance, bravery, humility, patience, and hard work. Endurance was taught to children by expecting them to stay in sweat lodges all day and withstand hot temperatures or go into frigid waters for cleansing. These values were integral to living in balance in a collective, cooperative society. Practical activities such as hunting, fishing, and berry picking taught them cooperation, sharing, self-awareness, and good judgment (Billy, 2009).

Young men and women received spiritual training for several years, called *etsxé7* to teach them the practical skills and spiritual beliefs of the Secwépemc society (Billy, 2009). Training in fasting, cleansing, and praying, which were all components of the education of children, signified a call to adulthood. Children were encouraged to play physically to strengthen their bodies (Jules, 1996). Boys, around the time their voices changed, spent several months alone in the wilderness to fend for themselves (Coffey et al., 1990). Boys were trained by fasting, cleansing in cold water, engaging in heavy physical activity, learning to understand nature, and living off the land. They developed "self-discipline, courage, patience, endurance, as well as mental, physical, and spiritual strength" (Billy, 2009, p. 177). This was rigorous mental training.

Girls also participated in etsxé7. Before their first menses, girls were secluded and taught skills and values that would be needed throughout their lives (Billy, 2009). They were required to gather boughs and pick up needles, which gave them the skills to become fast berry pickers. This also helped them develop patience and perseverance.

Storytelling was integral to the Secwépemc culture. Developing self-respect was an important lesson. The story of sockeye salmon was told to youth to explain the changes in their bodies. The sockeye's bodies changed according to the seasons, just as the bodies of children change as they approach adolescence. In the story of the sockeye, adolescents learned to develop self-respect by accepting these changes as a normal and natural part of development (Billy, 2009).

Indigenous wellness was based on the balance and synergy between physical, spiritual, emotional, and mental health (Hart, 2002). Youth learned important lessons to build their strengths and values. Perseverance, self-reliance, cooperation, and self-respect were taught through life skills practices, ceremonies, and stories. The value of generosity was instilled in all youth in ceremonial ways such as giving away their first kill or the first berries they picked (Billy, 2009). The people were strong and healthy; there was virtually no diabetes or dental cavities (FNHA, 2022). However, the arrival of Europeans changed the ways of the Indigenous people, and their traditional ways of living were destroyed. This had a detrimental effect on their health and well-being.

Effects of Colonization on Health

Prior to colonization, it was estimated that between 200,000 and more than a million Indigenous people lived in British Columbia (Boyd, 1990, as cited in Ignace & Ignace, 2017). After colonization, an estimated 80 percent of the Indigenous population was wiped out due to smallpox, diphtheria, pneumonia, measles, tuberculosis, whooping cough, and other diseases (Coffey et al., 1990). Those left behind were broken and devastated. With the collapse of the population, many of the traditional healing practices were lost or repressed by the European settlers (FNHA, 2022). Traditional healers were ineffective in treating the new diseases, and they themselves often perished (FNHA, 2022). As a result, traditional healing practices were often not taught to younger generations. In addition, Indigenous people were often denied Western health care; they were often confined to live on reserves in substandard conditions in overpopulated villages, which increased health risks.

Being confined to a reserve disrupted the people's relationship to the land. Because they could no longer hunt, fish, and gather, Indigenous people were forced to eat European food and were introduced to flour, sugar, and other foreign products that affected their physical health (FNHC, 2011). Many starved because of the inadequate nutrition. Obesity and other ailments began to emerge, and people's body types transformed from being lean and healthy to overweight and sickly. Alcohol use became more widespread, which led to additional problems (FNHA, 2022). The loss of culture and tradition meant a people, without their traditional ways and identity, became lost and bereft.

The mental and emotional health of Indigenous people was further damaged when children were removed from their community and indoctrinated into the church and Western ways of living in Indian residential schools. The children were forced to wear European clothing, not allowed to practice any cultural traditions, and forbidden to speak their mother tongue, even with their siblings. Their mental and emotional health was further affected by abuses they experienced at the residential schools (FNHA, 2022). Many children died of malnourishment, disease, and abuse. Many never returned home to their families. This led to a separation of their identity and ways of living and being. Children are the centre of traditional Secwépemc culture, and when the government took their children and put them into residential schools, they took the heart out of the community (Brendtro et al., 1990).

When residential schools denied children their families, and families their children, connections, love, and security were lost. The children, growing up without the nurturing of their family and community, experienced a disconnection from love and compassion (Haig-Brown, 1988). Sometimes the institution purposefully impaired the children's ability to feel and express emotions by strapping them and not allowing them to show emotions or cry (1988).

Colonization oppressed Indigenous people who suffered a great loss of their ancestral philosophies and traditions (Jules, 1996). This did not only affect the residential school survivors, but also their descendants, and their descendants, resulting in intergenerational trauma (Duran, 2006).

Decolonization is necessary to promote healing and reconciliation.

Decolonization

> Decolonizing actions must begin in the mind, and that creative, consistent, decolonized thinking shapes and empowers the brain, which in turn provides a major prime for positive change. (Waziyatawin & Yellow Bird, 2012, p. 2)

Decolonization requires Indigenous people to resist the colonizers and embrace their traditional ways while rejecting the Western ways in which they were indoctrinated (Waziyatawin & Yellow Bird, 2012). Decolonization is the resistance to colonialism—to the "exploitation of our minds, bodies, and lands" (p. 3). Colonization resulted in the loss of self-determination and traditional ways, which caused poverty, family separations, disease, and social problems. Liberation occurs when the people resist colonization. Decolonization is not passive; it requires action for transformation to occur. Decolonization requires Indigenous people to reclaim the "intellectual knowledge of Indigenous communities' healers and to reassert Indigenous epistemologies and ontologies" (Clark, 2016, p. 7). The minds of the colonizers must also be transformed so they are able to recognize the pervasive institutional racism evident in many components of society and in the health care system.

The mental health system is one area where Indigenous people continue to be oppressed. "Psychological oppression" (Duran et al., 2008, p. 288) happens when professionals perpetuate injustice and institutional racism by imposing culturally inappropriate practices, which are not congruent with Indigenous world views and traditional practices. Many Western approaches to mental health care expect clients to participate in a certain way, which continues to marginalize those whose world views are not in balance with Western approaches. More harm can be done than good. Counsellors, if they want to work with Indigenous clients, "will need to undertake a serious self-examination of the impact of their privileged position in society that often leads them to ignore many of [*sic*] injustices that underlie clients' soul wounds and psychological distress" (2008, p. 289).

These professionals would benefit their clients by adopting epistemological hybridity, which is to become "enmeshed in the cultural lifeworld of the person or community seeking help" (2008, p. 291). To do so, helping professionals need to unpack "privilege, whiteness, oppression, colonialism, racism, and marginalization" to look honestly inwards (Hart, 2014, p. 82). It is about creating relationships with Indigenous people to develop cultural sensitivity and awareness and to learn about Indigenous world views to become competent in safe practice.

Yellow Bird et al. (2020) discussed ways to increase cultural sensitivity and awareness to unpack privilege and become an "ally" to fight against systemic racism. They suggest the practice of mindfulness, which focuses on the present-moment experience with acceptance and non-judgment (Kabat-Zinn, 2013), as it can bring awareness of implicit biases and racism. Yellow Bird et al. (2020) advocate adopting decolonized mindfulness, which incorporates an open-minded approach of looking within to honestly and mindfully become aware of white privilege, and to deeply understand how one has contributed to systemic racism and remained complacent and inactive to injustice. Mindfulness and compassion have become tools to engage in collective anti-racist work, to unpack implicit biases, and to empower people to become active against systemic racism. Decolonized mindfulness can "bring a more radical, activist mindfulness to all participants who seek positive, loving, and radical change" (Yellow Bird et al., 2020, para. 3).

Liberation psychology is the awareness of cultural oppression and social injustices in the mental health field caused by Western-trained mental health practitioners (Duran at al., 2008). "According to Freire, the transformation of the oppressor as well as the oppressed involves a genuine act of love that has profound implications for the work in which counsellors are supposed to be engaged within a culturally diverse contemporary society" (p. 289). The oppressors can use mindfulness to be aware of implicit biases and institutional racism. The oppressed can use mindfulness to empower themselves and decolonize their minds.

Wilson and Yellow Bird discussed how mindfulness leads to what they term "neurodecolonization" (2005, as cited in Yellow Bird, 2013).

Neurodecolonization is a process in which "creative, healthy, decolonized thinking, actions and feelings positively shape and empower important neural circuits in our brain, which, in turn, provide us with the personal resources, strengths, talents and abilities we need to overcome and transform the oppressions of colonialism" (Yellow Bird, 2012, as cited in Yellow Bird, 2013, p. 293). Neurodecolonization, then, is being aware of the debilitating effects of colonization, acknowledging them in a healthy way, and transforming thoughts into compassion and the courage to change the way things are. However, to facilitate action for decolonization, there must be more than awareness; there must be a liberating force to transform the way things are (Freire, 1970). Decolonization requires "praxis" or action, which is "reflection and action upon the world in order to transform it" (p. 51). Indigenous traditional health practices need to be legitimized.

To work with Indigenous peoples, helping professionals need to have knowledge of both Western and Indigenous ways of knowing. The word "psychology" means the "study of soul" (Duran, 2006, p. 19); thus, psychotherapists can be considered "soul healers." Psychotherapists who work with Indigenous people need to become culturally competent to understand intergenerational trauma or the wounding of the soul, so they stop blaming the victim. Furthermore, helping professionals must understand that a whole culture has been wounded.

Indigenous Views of Wellness

> All Our Relations Healing and Healthy Together (Secwépemc Health Caucus, 2022)

Indigenous ways of healing are flourishing again and being sought by non-Indigenous as well as Indigenous people (Hart, 2014). Indigenous populations are on the rebound; infant mortality rates are dropping, and diseases are as well. It is one of the fastest growing populations in BC (FNHA, 2022). Wellness, from the Indigenous perspective, is a balance and synergy among four components: body, mind, emotions, and spirit (McCabe, 2008). Indigenous teachings involve keeping a balance between these four elements or directions, which means "wholeness, relationship, balance and harmony" (Hart, 2014, p. 77). Indigenous people are connected with community and land; however, this holistic healing model is ignored in the Western health care system (Clark, 2018). Wellness in many traditional Indigenous cultures means living in balance with nature, whereas wellness in Western cultures is the absence of disease or disorders (Duran et al., 2008).

A Western diagnosis is not congruent with Indigenous world views. Duran (2006) stated that a clinical diagnosis has been considered a type of naming ceremony by Indigenous people. In essence, they may consider their diagnosis part of their identity, and they may refer to themselves not by their name, but by their diagnosis.

In some traditional Indigenous healing practices, the naming of the sickness is intended to create a new relationship with the illness, which creates harmony with the illness. Clements (1932, as cited in Duran, 2006) discussed "object intrusion" (p. 6) as the concept that an object has invaded the body. For example, depression can be described as "the sadness has entered a person" instead of being considered something a person has. Therapy is intended to extract the object from the person. Another concept is "loss of soul," when the person becomes depersonalized or loses contact with reality. Duran et al. (2008) discussed the concept of the "soul wound" (p. 289) as intergenerational trauma, the unresolved trauma passed down through the generations which becomes cumulative. As a result, the trauma becomes more severe the longer it is unresolved (Duran, 2006). The Indigenous understanding is that the trauma occurs in the soul or spirit. "From an Indigenous liberation psychology perspective, individuals can be very depressed and still have a relationship with their soul and the way their soul harmonizes with the universal life force" (Duran et al., 2008, p. 293). In this way, the problem can be seen as something at one moment in time rather than defining a person; the client can seek to find a way to relieve the sadness or find a new relationship with the sadness to find balance. The person can look back into their history to identify when this sadness occurred. In addition, a ceremony can be performed to release the sadness. A new naming ceremony needs to be performed to offer the person a new identity that liberates them from the colonizing diagnosis.

Indigenous healing is promoted through belonging or connectedness (McCormick & Amundson, 1997), which means attaining or maintaining connection with sources of meaning and guidance beyond the self, such as family, community, culture, nation, the natural world, and the spiritual world. Relationships are the interconnection between people, animals, land, and spirits. "We must nurture the relationships we have with ourselves, with other people, with other animals, with the elements and with the spiritual realm. We refer to these others as our "relations" (Hart, 2014, p. 75). "All my relations" means that everything is connected—the stars, the universe, the earth, and every creature, including humans. Child well-being and healing practices, relationships, and kinship are "rooted in ceremonies and relationship to the land" (Clark, 2018, p. 15). Traditional ceremonies and practices such as sweat lodge ceremonies, dances, pipes, fasting, vision quests, and smudging continue to be important Indigenous healing practices. The sweat lodge supports a connection to the spiritual world, healing, and personal growth (Hart, 2014). Even though vision quests often seem like a solitary action, "it happens in the context of the community and the land" (Clark, 2018, p. 16). Participating in ceremony helps to develop values of respect, honesty, kindness, humility, sharing, and thankfulness (Hart, 2002).

Connection means connecting to ancestors and traditional knowledge, which are handed down through the generations, contributing to community well-being (Hart, 2014). Ways of knowing are important to hand down to future generations through knowledge keepers (Clark, 2018). Indigenous knowledge keepers are recognized people in the community who have gifts and contribute to the well-being of the community. Elders, traditional teachers, medicine people, and spiritual advisors teach support healing and growth through story (Hart, 2014). Elders are role models, recognized by the community, who live out the cultural values.

Traditional healing strategies such as diet, intense physical activity, ceremonies, and interpersonal skills are practices in discipline, which can improve health and wellness (Billy, 2009). Activities such as dancing, storytelling, and meditative practices such as praying and listening deeply are practices based on teaching discipline (Hart, 2014).

Cleansing practices are also used in healing. Cleansing means identifying and expressing emotions in a good way (Hart, 2014). Fasting is a method of healing and growth which usually lasts about four days, where a person gains spiritual insight, connection, self-awareness, and knowledge (Hart, 2014). Smudging is another method of cleansing that often occurs during ceremonies or other events. Plants such as sage are dried and lit to create smoke, which is gently washed over a person. "This cleanses the mind, heart, body and spirit" (Hart, 2014, p. 80). Smoke takes a person's thoughts and feelings to a higher power. When having a bad day, using water for cleaning by going for a cold dip or sitting under a "red willow tree takes away negative emotions" (Billy, 2009, p. 204).

New approaches are needed for interventions and training for health care professionals working with Indigenous people. Wise practices grounded in oral histories use many traditional healing interventions such as Elder's teachings, storytelling, language programs, land-based activities, fasting, and powwows, traditional art forms, harvesting medicines, drumming, singing, and dancing. No single Indigenous best-practice approach can be used because Indigenous communities are so different from each other (Clark, 2016). What is required are safe spaces to address health needs, to address institutional racism, and to meet the needs of the Indigenous populations through a holistic, strength-based framework.

Indigenous Wellness Programs for Youth

Clark stated that youth programs need to be aligned with Indigenous values, paradigms, and epistemologies based on strengths, resistance, and survivance, which are "wise practices" (2016, p. 7). Her research shows that Indigenous youth who have strong connections to their community have improved educational achievement and self-esteem, and they partake less in risky drug and sex activities (Clark, 2016). Clark further found that 96 percent of the Indigenous youth in her study were proud to identify as Indigenous, and those who spoke their language and practised their culture and traditions rated their health as highest. In addition, McCormick (2009) found that youth with a strong cultural identity were better able to recover from suicidal thoughts and ideation.

Clark stated that "resistance communities" are essential for healing for Indigenous children and youth (2016, p. 9). Resistance strategies will create a strong sense of self that enables people to free themselves from colonizing effects. According to Billy, "We need knowledge on appropriate emotional healing techniques and practices which will help release intergenerational trauma and increase self-esteem and self-confidence" (2009, p. 215). McCormick (2009) sought to find out what strategies were used to help Aboriginal people heal. Some of these were participating in ceremonies, expressing emotion, learning from a role model, establishing a connection with nature, doing exercise, engaging in challenging activities, establishing a social connection, gaining an understanding of the problem, establishing a spiritual connection, obtaining help and support from others, doing self-care, setting goals, anchoring the self in tradition, and helping others. Many of these practices have been integrated into Indigenous youth programs.

Clark (2018) described her work with Indigenous girls' groups as promoting resilience and resistance. Through storytelling and witnessing, the girls were given the space to discuss their experiences in safe and non-threatening ways. The girls were introduced to traditional "rites of passage" (p. 67) facilitated by Elders to explore key issues in their lives. The girls were supported to have healthy resistance to systemic problems such as racism, sexism, and poverty.

Brave Heart et al. (2012) discussed an intervention for youth called RezRIDERS. It is an extreme sport experiential education intervention designed to reduce substance abuse and depression. In this intervention, youth engage in challenging activities to promote healthy prosocial activities to shift them away from high-risk activities. Youth work in teams on community projects and activities to build community and ecological responsibility. Trust-building exercises are used to encourage positive prosocial relationships. The program incorporates traditional customs and healing practices to address intergenerational trauma and discuss important topics.

Waziyatawin and Yellow Bird (2012) used mindfulness to connect with youth. Mindfulness practices allowed the youth to be aware of how intergenerational trauma has affected them. This awareness is the beginning of acceptance and of being able to address how trauma has manifested in their bodies and minds. Waziyatawin and Yellow Bird found that mindfulness practices helped youth to overcome depression and allowed them to be more optimistic about their future.

Adults as well as youth require wellness programs grounded in wise practices based on traditional healing practices. Many of these practices should be integrated into the existing health care system, not only because of the Truth and Reconciliation Calls to Action but also because they are good practices in health care. Specifically, for Indigenous peoples in Canada, health care practitioners require knowledge based on holistic health care practices grounded in Indigenous culture. Health care practitioners require training in Indigenous health care practices to better serve the Indigenous community. One Elder recently stated that there are not enough of them around anymore that know the traditional ways; therefore, more people need to be trained. Strength-based practices with the foundation of health and wellness, compassion for ourselves and others, and care for our environment, is what will help us move forward.

References

Billy, J. (2009). *Back from the brink: Decolonizing through the restoration of Secwépemc language, culture, and identity* [Unpublished doctoral dissertation]. Simon Fraser University.

Brave Heart, M. Y., Elkins, J., Tafoya, G., Bird, D., & Salvador, M. (2012). Wicasa Was'aka: Restoring the traditional strength of American Indian boys and men. *American Journal of Public Health*, 102(2), 177–183.

Brendtro, L. K., Brokenleg, M., & Van Bockern, S. (1990). *Reclaiming youth at risk: Our hope for the future*. National Educational Service.

Clark, N. (2016). Shock and awe: Trauma as the new colonial frontier. *Humanities*, 5(14), 1–16.

Clark, N. (2018). *Cu7 me7 a'wele'wu-kt. "Come on, let's go berry-picking." Revival of Secwépemc wellness approaches for healing Indigenous child and youth experiences of violence* [Unpublished doctoral dissertation]. Simon Fraser University.

Coffey, J., Goldstrom, E., Gottfriedson, G., Matthew, R., & Walton, P. (1990). *Shuswap history: The first 100 years of contact*. Secwepemc Cultural Education Society.

Duran, E. (2006). *Healing the soul wound: Counseling with American Indians and other native peoples*. Teachers College Press.

Duran, E., Firehammer, J., & Gonzalez, J. (2008). Liberation psychology as the path toward healing cultural soul wounds. *Journal of Counseling and Development*, 86, 288–295.

First Nations Health Authority [FNHA]. (2022). *Our history, our health. Wellness and the FNHA*. https://www.fnha.ca/wellness/wellness-for-first-nations/our-history-our-health

First Nations Health Council [FNHC]. (2011). *Implementing the vision: BC First Nations health governance*. First Nations Health Council. https://www.fnha.ca/Documents/FNHC_Health_Governance_Book.pdf

Freire, P. (1970). *Pedagogy of the oppressed*. (M. B. Ramos, Trans.). Continuum International Publishing.

Haig-Brown, C. (1988). *Resistance and renewal: Surviving the Indian residential school*. Arsenal Pulp Press.

Hart, M. A. (2002). *Seeking Mino-Pimatisiwin: An Aboriginal approach to healing*. Fernwood Publishing.

Hart, M. A. (2014). Indigenous ways of helping. In Menzies, P., & Lavalee, L. F. (Eds.), *Journey to healing: Aboriginal people with addiction and mental health issues: What health, social service and justice workers need to know* (pp.73–86). Centre for Addiction and Mental Health.

Ignace, M., & Ignace, R. (2017). *Secwépemc people, land, and law: Yerí7 Re Stsq'ey's-kucw*. McGill-Queen's University Press.

Jules, D. M. (1996). *Traditional ways Shuswap people identified and nurtured gifted and talented girls: Shuswap eminent women tell their stories* [Unpublished master's thesis]. University of British Columbia.

Kabat-Zinn, J. (2013). *Full catastrophe living: Using the wisdom of your body and mind to face stress, pain, and illness*. Bantam Books.

McCabe, G. (2008). Mind, body, emotions and spirit: Reaching to the ancestors for healing. *Counselling Psychology Quarterly*, 21(2), 143–152.

McCormick, R. (2009). Aboriginal Approaches to Counselling. In Kirmayer, L., &

Valaskakis, G. (Eds.), *Healing traditions: The mental health of aboriginal peoples in Canada* (pp. 337–354). UBC Press.

McCormick, R. M., & Amundson, N. E. (1997). A career-life planning model for first nations people. *Journal of Employment Counselling, 34*, 171–179.

National Centre for Truth and Reconciliation. (2022). *About.* https://nctr.ca/about/

Secwépemc Health Caucus. (2022). *Secwépemc Health Caucus home page.* https://secwepemchealth.ca/

Siegel, D. (2010). *Mindsight: The new science of personal transformation.* Bantam Books.

Truth and Reconciliation Commission of Canada [TRC]. (2015). *Truth and Reconciliation Commission of Canada: Calls to Action.* https://ehprnh2mwo3.exactdn.com/wp-content/uploads/2021/01/Calls_to_Action_English2.pdf

Turner, N. J. (2017). Re Styecwmenulecws-kucw: How we look(ed) after our land. In Ignace, M., & Ignace, R. (Eds.), *Secwépemc people, land, and laws: Yerí7 Re Stsq'ey's-kucw* (pp. 145–219). McGill-Queen's University Press.

Waziyatawin & Yellow Bird, M. (2012). Decolonizing our minds and actions. In Waziyatawin & Yellow Bird, M. (Eds.), *For indigenous minds only: A decolonization handbook* (pp. 1–14). School of Advanced Research Press.

Yellow Bird, M. (2013). Neurodecolonization: Applying mindfulness research to decolonizing social work. In Gray, T., Coates, J., Yellow Bird, M., & Hetherington, T. (Eds.), *Decolonizing social work* (pp. 293–310). Ashgate Publishing Limited.

Yellow Bird, M., Gehl, M., Hatton-Bowers, H., Hicks, L. J., & Reno-Smith, D. (2020, October 30). *Defunding mindfulness: While we sit on our cushions, systemic racism runs rampant.* Zero to Three. https://www.zerotothree.org/resource/journal/perspectives-defunding-mindfulness-while-we-sit-on-our-cushions-systemic-racism-runs-rampant/#chapter-3055

EDUCATION FOR RECONCILIATION CALLS TO ACTION

The Truth and Reconciliation Commission (2015, pp. 7–8) made four Calls to Action in relation to Education for Reconciliation. Issues named as priorities for change in relation to Education for Reconciliation by the Calls to Action are:

62. We call upon the federal, provincial, and territorial governments, in consultation and collaboration with Survivors, Aboriginal peoples, and educators, to:
    i. Make age-appropriate curriculum on residential schools, Treaties, and Aboriginal peoples' historical and contemporary contributions to Canada a mandatory education requirement for Kindergarten to Grade Twelve students.
    ii. Provide the necessary funding to post-secondary institutions to educate teachers on how to integrate Indigenous knowledge and teaching methods into classrooms.
    iii. Provide the necessary funding to Aboriginal schools to utilize Indigenous knowledge and teaching methods in classrooms.
    iv. Establish senior-level positions in government at the assistant deputy minister level or higher dedicated to Aboriginal content in education.

63. We call upon the Council of Ministers of Education, Canada to maintain an annual commitment to Aboriginal education issues, including:
     i.   Developing and implementing Kindergarten to Grade Twelve curriculum and learning resources on Aboriginal peoples in Canadian history, and the history and legacy of residential schools.
     ii. Sharing information and best practices on teaching curriculum related to residential schools and Aboriginal history.
     iii. Building student capacity for intercultural understanding, empathy, and mutual respect.
     iv. Identifying teacher-training needs relating to the above.
64. We call upon all levels of government that provide public funds to denominational schools to require such schools to provide an education on comparative religious studies, which must include a segment on Aboriginal spiritual beliefs and practices developed in collaboration with Aboriginal Elders.
65. We call upon the federal government, through the Social Sciences and Humanities Research Council, and in collaboration with Aboriginal peoples, post-secondary institutions and educators, and the National Centre for Truth and Reconciliation and its partner institutions, to establish a national research program with multi-year funding to advance understanding of reconciliation.

References

Truth and Reconciliation Commission of Canada. (2015). *Truth and Reconciliation Commission of Canada: Calls to Action.* https://ehprnh2mwo3.exactdn.com/wp-content/uploads/2021/01/Calls_to_Action_English2.pdf

KIRS* Curriculum

Garry Gottfriedson

teach children
domestic skills

like how to hate
the opposite sex

like pruning trees
to blossom dysfunction

like planting seeds
to sprout self-loathing

like learning the word of god
on bent knees pleasing priests

like discovering death 215 times
multiplied infinitely

---

*   Kamloops Indian Residential School.

Change Begins with a Whisper

Georgann Cope Watson

Abstract

It is time for me to respond to the Truth and Reconciliation (TRC) Calls to Action in my personal and professional life. By extension, it is time for me to strive to decolonize my pedagogical practice. In this chapter, I draw upon four significant learning experiences from the past year to design an action plan to honour TRC Call to Action 62 ii, iii, and iv (Truth and Reconciliation Commission of Canada, 2015, p. 7). The purpose of this project is to integrate Indigenous ways of knowing and Indigenous pedagogies into the curriculum of the online courses I teach. The action plan is the practical application of this research, which, once disseminated, has implications for my personal practice and implications for other educators who may find resonance with the findings.

Searching: A Journey Toward Reconcili*action*

Searching

> In the forest, in my mind
> Looking for space
> Between, amongst, through trees
> A path
> That guides
> Brilliant colours
> And swooshing sounds

Sometimes soft
Other times harsh
Always alive

        Searching for space, searching for self

        Space for
        Understanding
        Time carries on slowly
        With patience and searches
        For new ways
        Like trees that renew
        In Spring

Wandering, wondering
Guided by noises of trees
Softly whispering
A way
Finding self
Learning takes time and patience
Following ribbons
Of the path
To knowing

        Thinking, Listening
        Shifting shapes of trees
        Ring with
        Sounds of hope
        Searching, finding, changing
        Always a path
        Answers in the forest
        Find them there
        Listen
        Change begins with a whisper

I wish to acknowledge that the land on which I reside is within the Ktunaxa traditional territory and is the homeland of the Ktunaxa people. The Ktunaxa people have always been here. Historically, other Indigenous peoples also harvested, hunted, fished, and settled seasonally within the area, including the Secwépemc peoples who for centuries have travelled to and inhabited the Ktunaxa homelands. Previously, I lived on the unceded territory of Secwépemc First Nation in Secwepemcúlecw. I think of myself as a visitor on these traditional lands. I share this information as an acknowledgement of my settler status.

The problem addressed in this study stems from my lived experience as a Canadian citizen with very little knowledge of Indigenous history, culture, beliefs, and pedagogies. In this chapter I address this problem through a process of reconcili*action* (reconciliation in action) (National Centre for Truth and Reconciliation, n.d.). I have been studying, listening, and reflecting on the history of colonization in Canada for two decades. I have taken courses, participated in Massive Open Online Courses (MOOC), attended workshops, read books and articles, visited sites and attended ceremonies, and completed research studies to build knowledge and discover truths. I have been thinking about, and talking about, Indigenization, but I have not made any significant progress toward reconcili*action*. It is now time for me to act and, by extension, decolonize myself and my pedagogical practice. My positionality as a settler and my lens as a university professor must be considered in this work. I speak from a privileged space filtered through my lived experience as a member of the dominant social group and I acknowledge that a reflexive approach threads through this chapter.

The purpose of this chapter is to develop and to share an action plan to respond to TRC Call to Action 63 ii, iii, and iv. I first share my personal journey to this moment to provide some background to the particular focus I bring to this project and to situate my positionality as part of the dominant group. Next, I draw upon four significant learning experiences from the past year that informed this project of decolonization and integration of Indigenous pedagogies into the curriculum of the online courses I teach. I share an action plan as the practical application of this research, which, once disseminated, has implications for my personal practice and implications for other educators as they may find resonance with this research.

A Personal Journey

I had a lot to learn. My personal journey to reconciliation began many decades ago. I was raised in Niagara, Ontario, in a small town that served as a bedroom community for nearby industrialized cities. I had a charmed life, filled with clichés including many middles: middle class, middle town, middle child, middle student. In reflection, I lived on a boulevard of green lights, holding unearned advantage and conferred dominance, terms introduced by McIntosh (1989) in their seminal work on white privilege. I remember thinking at a very young age how lucky I was to have white skin.

FIGURE 3.1. The conversation with Georgann Cope Watson (on screen), Garry Gottfriedson, and Sarah Ladd.
Source: Victoria Handford.

This thought was the beginning of a long path to search for a sense of place regarding my positionality.

I carried with me a deficit ideology regarding Indigenous peoples, having been socialized to believe in white supremacy. Gorski (2011) describes the deficit ideology as a perspective that approaches others with a perception of inherent weakness rather than strength. I was guilty of stereotyping, carrying unexplored bias, holding false assumptions, and following the false narratives around Indigenous people as truth. I lived near the largest reserve in Canada, the Six Nations of the Grand River Reserve, yet I knew nothing about the people who lived there. Indigenous history was not part of the curriculum throughout the 1960s and 1970s. I had little impetus to engage in self-directed learning to fill this knowledge gap and did not know or interact with any Indigenous peoples through these years.

In the early 1980s, I moved to Alberta, filled with wonder over a romanticized vision of ranches, horses, and a cowboy lifestyle. I began to notice the presence of Indigenous peoples, something that, for me, was missing in Ontario. A move further west to the coast of British Columbia brought about a greater awareness of Indigenous culture, language, history, and knowledge. I became more engaged in learning about the history of colonization, continuing oppression, and Indian residential school system (IRSS). I knew enough to know a little, but not enough to know a lot. I never thought of myself as a settler, a colonizer, or a participant in any way in this part of Canadian history. I was entrenched in the cliché that colonization was something that happened in the past and had nothing to do with me and my actions.

In the 1990s, I enrolled our son in a preschool program on the nearby reserve, mostly because it was affordable and because a bus picked him up at my door. I was being a "good" white person, a construct I held on to. I thought a bit about what he was learning, but never really engaged in any deep or reflective knowledge regarding colonization. At the same time, I taught a parenting program called Nobody's Perfect, and tried to reproduce the program for Indigenous people that I had previously facilitated for non-Indigenous people. This disorienting experience stimulated my first reflective thinking about the cultural differences and cultural values of Indigenous peoples. Everything I did at that program was wrong: the food, the childcare, the agenda, the textbooks and resources, and the facilitation style. I never went back to try again, but that experience stayed with me. I was searching for answers to why this workshop failed, but they could not surface because I lacked any depth of knowledge of Indigenous history, culture, and pedagogies.

Later, I began to learn more about Indigenous people through personal relationships and discovery. When I moved to a small town near Kamloops, BC, I learned more about the IRSS. It is impossible to live in Kamloops and not feel the presence of the school, which is front and centre. At night, the ground is up-lit, providing an eerie view of the building and stimulating thoughts about the secrets held within its walls. In 2021, the discovery of 215 unmarked graves at this school has changed everything. But in the 1990s, I did not know anything about Secwépemc First Nation or the atrocities of the IRSS.

My real search for knowing began in the early 2000s, when I was a teaching assistant in an Introduction to Women's Studies course. Finally, Indigenous history was included in the curriculum. An assignment on the IRSS and the Sixties Scoop was part of the course. This set me searching for knowledge because teaching the course required intensive study and an exploration of the historical context of colonization. At the same time, I encouraged my daughter, a Grade 11 student, to write a paper on the IRSS for her socials course, and the search for knowing materialized. Since then,

I have been a student of Indigenous history, culture, beliefs, and pedagogies in my search for knowing. This chapter is the next step: reconcili*action*.

Reflections on Learning Experiences

I draw upon four recent experiences with Indigenous educators, which inform a plan for addressing the TRC Call to Action 62 ii, iii, and iv. First, I draw on my experience and learning at the American Association of Curriculum and Teaching (AACT) conference in October 2021, which I had searched for to learn more about Indigenous pedagogies and culturally responsive curriculum in the United States. I attended four important sessions: Pedagogies of Purpose: Awakening Critical Consciousness (White and Flynn); Honouring-Not-Exploiting Native Americans (Mennom et al.), Creativity in an Indigenous Land (Migizi Gwiiwizens); and the Kyilka Lecture by Dr. Gregory Cajete. Cajete spoke of culturally responsive curricula geared to the special needs and learning styles of Native American students, based upon the Native American understanding of the "nature of nature." This lecture was a highlight of my experience and helped forge a path of understanding for me.

At the AACT conference, I was an outsider. I was the only participant from Canada and was identified by the language I was using (i.e., Indigenous vs. Native American), my perspective on Indigenization (i.e., the TRC Calls to Action is a Canadian document), and my perspective on race relations, (i.e., Indigenous, Black and People of Colour—IBPOC vs. Black, Indigenous, and People of Colour—BIPOC). In the first session I attended, I asked scholars to speak to the ban on teaching Critical Race Theory in K–12 education in some US states. My intention was to explore the ideas of educators faced with this ban, as I saw parallels with teaching about the atrocities and genocide committed by the IRSS. I heard their frustrations, particularly from those committed to social justice education and the telling of truth. This discussion helped me to situate the context of denying space for truth. The students I teach, who are mostly (but not all) in-service teachers, often say that they do not know where to start with Indigenization or that they are worried about how much to share with the young students they teach. I could see that there was a lack of professional development on teaching truth, and that this was a curricular gap that might be something I could address in the graduate courses I teach.

In his keynote address, Cajete told a story of the gentle but determined path he took to create culturally responsive pedagogies geared toward the special needs and learning styles of Native American students. The curricula are based upon Native American understanding of the nature of nature and utilizes this foundation to develop an understanding of the science and artistic thought process as expressed in Indigenous perspective of the natural world (Cajete, 2021).

In this story, I heard important points that engaged my interest. For example, Indigenous epistemologies are grounded in four spheres: self-to-self; self-to-family; self-to-community; and self-to-cosmos. It is important to take the strengths within the four spheres and use them to reconnect through stories that share inner experiences and self-knowledge. Cajete said that meaningful connections for life are created by authentic experiences. According to him, students in higher education are looking for change, administration is resisting this change, but curriculum can be used as an anti-racist tool, and to "create new ways to understand curriculum, ignite the spark, look to the mountain" (Cajete, 2021). I bring these ideas forward in the process of reconcili*action*.

In the fall of 2021, I attended a four-part learning colloquium with educator Jo Chrona, a member of the First Nations Education Steering Committee who shares and teaches the nine First Peoples Principles of Learning. During this colloquium, I recognized that Canada has a systemic ignorance about Indigenous people, and that ignoring the colonial histories and legacies would lead to a proliferation of colonizing practices and reproduction of oppressive systems based in racism. The foundation for this series was anti-racist work, something I had been engaged in for many years. Chrona (personal communication, 2021) asked: "What specifically do we need to do to engage in anti-racist work?" I felt resonance with Cajete's words. His question prompted a commitment to move teaching into places of discomfort, a place to support each other's growth. Chrona also highlighted the concept of epistemic racism, a form of racism that prioritizes particular knowledge systems and pushes other knowledge systems to the margins. I could see that happening in my history, my practice, and my institution. I thought about the ways in which systemic ignorance acted as a barrier to reconciliation, and my need to answer the call Marie Wilson made at the Congress of the Humanities and Social Sciences in 2019. At her keynote address, Wilson demanded that every person in the room read the TRC documents and facilitate a process where all Canadians would do the same.

Another insight I gained from Chrona was around the idea of racist gaslighting. Phrases such as "I will play devil's advocate" or "In my opinion" or "Is it possible that…" are examples of remarks that people use to avoid truth and defer to the false narrative. I learned how to speak back to these actions in ways that do not avoid hard truths. For example, in a conversation around the discovery of 215 unmarked graves at the Kamloops Residential School site in 2021, someone suggested that there were most likely wooden crosses to mark graves but that those crosses had deteriorated. After the Chrona workshop, I was able to respond to that comment in a way that prioritized truth, explaining that truth had been revealed and that creating counter stories was a practice of denial that diminished the reality of the events of the 215 graves of children.

Chrona also addressed the practice of conflating multicultural education with Indigenous education. I learned that ignoring colonial histories and legacies, including stolen lands, languages, culture, and children, could not be seen as the same experiences for immigrants. Immigrants still had language, land, and culture that had not been erased. The histories were different. This was a significant learning moment for me, as the students I teach often try to conflate multicultural education with Indigenous education.

More recently, I attended two presentations by Laura Grizzlypaws, educational developer, Indigenous Teaching and Learning at Thompson Rivers University. The first presentation was on creating authentic and transformative land acknowledgements. Performing land acknowledgements has become a common practice in educational as well as many other contexts. However, some people recite the land acknowledgement as though checking off an item on a list, something Pidgeon (2016) writes about in their article on avoiding superficial practices without real connection to Indigenous knowledge, place, or history. Grizzlypaws opened with the following:

> Land Acknowledgement opens a space with gratefulness. It allows us to publicly recognize the Indigenous peoples whose traditional lands we stand upon. Land Acknowledgement honours past and present Indigenous stewardship of the natural world. It also offers respect and visibility for the histories, contributions, innovations, and contemporary perspectives of Indigenous peoples. As we gather in our institutions, businesses, and communities, we must realize that we all stand upon the work of Indigenous peoples in each and every place we move within. (2021)

During this workshop, I gained a deeper understanding of this decolonizing practice. First, I learned that the land acknowledgement honoured time immemorial, and that this countered the narrative that the land had been discovered. I once heard: "In 1492, Native Americans found Christopher Columbus floating aimlessly off the coast of their land." This made sense

to me. I also resonated with the land acknowledgement as an act of reconciliation, and an impetus to learn more about the traditional lands on
which I reside. Recently, I moved from the unceded traditional territory
of Secwépemc peoples to the traditional lands of Ktunaxa First Nation.
I am ashamed to admit it was a few months before I researched how to
pronounce "Ktunaxa" or explored the history of the peoples and the land.
All the information was readily available, but I had not considered this
act of reconciliation. Similarly, when I am asked how to pronounce an
Indigenous name or territory, I simply respond: "This information is available to you." I see these shortcomings as reminders that colonization is
ongoing, and that to decolonize, I must begin with myself.

The second presentation by Grizzlypaws was titled "Indigenous Land-
Based Teaching and Learning." Grizzlypaws taught us that

> land-based learning builds community connectedness and resilience,
> improves mental, physical, emotional, and spiritual wellness, advances recon-
> ciliation by decolonizing educational institutions, and improves our under-
> standing of land, territory, and the language of Indigenous peoples. (2022)

Grizzlypaws's presentation helped me pull together the ideas I had on land-
based and place-based learning. In a previous study, I had reflected on my
relationship with the land. I discovered that there were only a few moments
in my life where I felt a true connection to the land and the significance of
caring for it. This was a deep disconnect that I could not account for, and as
such, I was troubled by my inability to understand Indigenous land-based
learning and context. During this presentation, as Grizzlypaws storied the
circle of life around the salmon, I began to understand Indigenous pedagogies. This story made sense to me. I now had an opening for deeper concep-
tualizations of land-based learning.

The final learning experience was based in Garry Gottfriedson's
seven-week faculty seminar during the early months of 2022. All the participants were members of the staff and faculty of the same university, and,
as such, were colleagues. This created an immediate learning community,
and I felt it was a safe space to explore my own thoughts, insights, and
actions around the TRC Calls to Action. For me, it was a transformational
learning experience, as I addressed a disorienting dilemma (the search
for knowing) in a way that entails action, what I have come to consider
reconcili*action*. During the course, I listened in earnest to the knowledge
shared by Gottfriedson and began to understand the TRC Calls to Action
in a new and practical way. The first question I thought about was: What

is a colonial perspective and why is it still alive and well? This prompted me to think about the ways that I was reproducing colonizing practices and about the ways I could interrupt these practices with new practices informed by Indigenous ways of knowing and pedagogies. This was a step toward decolonizing the self. I heard Taiaiake Alfred (Swiech, 2021) share that the academy could not be decolonized, because, well, it was the academy! But I could begin by decolonizing my self and some elements of my practice. This was encouraging. Gottfriedson warned against using the term "settler guilt" as a way to appease the present. The shift must be made toward understanding what colonizing practices are and how they manifest in teaching. I learned that it is impossible to break these practices if we do not know what they are.

The course culminated in a writing retreat that I attended virtually. Knowledge keepers and Elders as well as Indigenous colleagues were invited and spoke to our group. Elder Mike made a statement that really resonated with me: "Don't let it end here, let it begin." I could respond! It was time to stop following the more general progress on the TRC Calls to Action and to address at least one of the calls in my own practice. The search was coming to an end. I had engaged in two decades of searching for ways to engage with reconciliation, and it was now time for reconcili*action*.

Reconcili*action*: Addressing TRC Call 63 ii, iii, and iv

As a step toward reconciliation, I decided to address TRC Call to Action 63 ii, iii, and iv. I am in the privileged position of educating teachers because I teach and develop curriculum for a graduate program in education. Most, but not all, of the students I teach are in-service K–12 teachers. Other students may be social workers, nurses, outdoor educators, program leaders, and counsellors. As a course developer and professor, I can infuse acts of reconciliation, decolonization, and Indigenization into the curriculum and lessons. Many of the courses that I teach would benefit from a curricular and pedagogical response to Call to Action 63. For example, I teach a Philosophy of Education course, a Curriculum, Teaching, and Learning course, an Equity, Diversity and Inclusion course and a History of Education in BC course. Now is the perfect time for reconcili*action*. The action plan in Appendix 1 integrates a response to TRC Call to Action 63 ii, iii, and iv and the nine First Peoples Principles of Learning into one course through explicit learning outcomes, learning activities, and learning assessments. I also followed TRU's *Indigenous Checklist* (Centre for Excellence in

Learning and Teaching, 2021) and the University of Regina's "100 ways to Indigenize and Decolonize Academic Programs and Courses" (Pete, 2020).

The course I chose for this project is an online graduate-level course in the Master of Education Program. The course is "Diversity: Constructing Social Realities" and is described in the university calendar as follows:

> Students investigate fundamental questions about the relationship between education and society. Inequalities based on race, culture, language, social class, gender, sexual orientation, (dis)ability status, ethnicity or religion and how they are socially constructed in contemporary society are considered, in addition to how they operate in educational environments. Students identify the effects of these identity constructs on the educational experiences of students and how these constructs shape student access, achievement, and attainment. Students are challenged with the following questions: How do schools reproduce, reinforce, and challenge social inequalities? How do educational materials embrace inclusive approaches within the broader contexts of multiculturalism, globalization and cosmopolitanism? How can educators promote inclusive education that values diversity and equity? (Thompson Rivers University, n.d.)

Commitment and Future Research

I was part of a team that redeveloped this course in 2022/23, and I intended to initiate this action plan, or a similar version of this action plan. I could not change the learning outcomes or the assessments in the course, but I could change some of the learning activities, add readings and videos, and share other resources. This is my commitment to this project.

The practical implications of this chapter are clear: I have developed an action plan that addresses TRC Call to Action 63 ii, iii, and iv. This action plan considers the nine First Peoples Principles of Learning while integrating suggested practices from TRU and the University of Regina. I have also included some of the established learning activities in the course, with a few modifications for Indigenization. The broader implication is that this chapter may be useful for other educators as they strive to move from searching to knowing.

References

Archibald, J. (2008). *Indigenous storywork: Educating the heart, mind, body and spirit.* UBC Press.

Battiste, M. (2013). *Decolonizing education: Nourishing the learning spirit.* UBC Press.

Cajete, G. (2021, October 8). *Kysilka Lecture* [Keynote address]. American Association of Teaching and Curriculum 27th Annual Conference, Albuquerque, New Mexico, United States.

Centre for Excellence in Learning and Teaching. (2021). *Indigenization checklist.* Thompson Rivers University. https://www.tru.ca/__shared/assets/TRU_Indigenous_Checklist55118.pdf

Donald, D. (2012). Indigenous métissage: A decolonizing research sensibility. *International Journal of Qualitative Studies in Education, 25*(5), 533–555.

First Nations Education Steering Committee [FNESC]. (2006). The First Peoples principles of learning. https://www.fnesc.ca/first-peoples-principles-of-learning

Gorski, P. (2011). *Unlearning the deficit ideology and the scornful gaze: Thoughts on authenticating the class discourse in education.* In Ahlquist, R., Gorski, P., & Montano, T. (Eds.), *Assault on Kids: How Hyper-Accountability, Corporatization, Deficit Ideologies, and Ruby Payne Are Destroying Our Schools* (pp. 152–173). Peter Lang.

Gottfriedson, G. (2010). *Skin like mine.* Ronsdale Press.

Grizzlypaws, L. (2021, November). *How to create authentic and transformative land acknowledgements.* [Virtual Workshop].

Grizzlypaws, L. (2022, April). *Indigenous Land-Based Teaching and Learning* [Conference Presentation]. Open Learning Faculty Member Conference, Kamloops, BC, Canada.

Ignace, M., & Ignace, R. (2017). *Secwépemc people, land and laws: Yerí7 re Stsq'ey's-kucw.* McGill-Queen's University Press.

Joseph, B. (2018). *21 things you may not know about the Indian Act.* Indigenous Relations Press. 27th Annual Conference, Albuquerque, New Mexico, United States.

King, T. (2018). *The inconvenient Indian.* Anchor Canada.

Manuel, G., & Posluns, M. (1974). *The fourth world: An Indian reality.* University of Minnesota Press.

McIntosh, P. (1989, July/August). White privilege: Unpacking the invisible knapsack. *Peace and Freedom Magazine,* 10–12.

National Centre for Truth and Reconciliation. (n.d.). *ReconciliACTION Plans.* University of Manitoba. https://nctr.ca/reconciliaction-plans/

Pete, S. (2020). *100 ways to Indigenize and decolonize academic programs and courses.* University of Regina. https://www.uregina.ca/president/assets/docs/president-docs/indigenization/indigenize-decolonize-university-courses.pdf

Pidgeon, M. (2016, February 23). More than a checklist: Meaningful Indigenous inclusion in higher education. *Multidisciplinary Studies in Social Inclusion, 4*(1), 77–91. https://doi.org/10.17645/si.v4i1.436

Swiech, C. (Host). (2021, April 30). Episode 60 with political activist Taiaiake Alfred [Audio podcast episode]. In From the Depths of Darkness to the Light of Success. https://open.spotify.com/episode/74hXgssXeXDtGZMLlMUkwY?si=Q1e5Rhm UTU29NeWJiBAcHA&nd=1&dlsi=a4ae6258f76d4754

Thompson Rivers University. (n.d.). *EDUC 5041 Diversity: Constructing Social Realities* [Course listing]. tru.ca/campus/current/calendar/current/EDUC5041.htm

Truth and Reconciliation Commission of Canada. (2015). *Truth and Reconciliation Commission of Canada: Calls to Action.* https://ehprnh2mwo3.exactdn.com/wp-content/uploads/2021/01/Calls_to_Action_English2.pdf

Wagamese, R. (2012). *Indian horse.* Douglas & McIntyre Press.

BUSINESS AND RECONCILIATION CALLS TO ACTION

The Truth and Reconciliation Commission (2015, p. 10) made one Call to Action in relation to Business and Reconciliation. Issues named as priorities for change in relation to Business and Reconciliation by the Calls to Action are:

92. We call upon the corporate sector in Canada to adopt the *United Nations Declaration on the Rights of Indigenous Peoples* as a reconciliation framework and to apply its principles, norms, and standards to corporate policy and core operational activities involving Indigenous peoples and their lands and resources. This would include, but not be limited to, the following:

    i. Commit to meaningful consultation, building respectful relationships, and obtaining the free, prior, and informed consent of Indigenous peoples before proceeding with economic development projects.

    ii. Ensure that Aboriginal peoples have equitable access to jobs, training, and education opportunities in the corporate sector, and that Aboriginal communities gain long-term sustainable benefits from economic development projects.

iii. Provide education for management and staff on the history of Aboriginal peoples, including the history and legacy of residential schools, the *United Nations Declaration on the Rights of Indigenous Peoples*, Treaties and Aboriginal rights, Indigenous law, and Aboriginal-Crown relations. This will require skills-based training in intercultural competency, conflict resolution, human rights, and anti-racism.

References

Truth and Reconciliation Commission of Canada. (2015). *Calls to Action*. Winnipeg, Manitoba.   https://ehprnh2mwo3.exactdn.com/wp-content/uploads/2021/01/Calls_to_Action_English2.pdf

Too Much

Fitting into corporate molds
requires wringing oneself out
like a sponge.
Draining colours of spirit
and culture comfort
into a cold steel bucket.
Then.
Setting aside the bucket to receive
interview methods taught.
Drenched in sickly green corporate ooze.
Becoming someone else gets you the job.
Arriving greyed out,
preparing to wring the sponge dry.
Again.
Dipping back into that bucket
soaking up what was set aside,
trying to regain whole self.
Hoping the essence has not been lost.
Next.
Navigating ooze,
your feet sticking in muck,
battling colonial processes from inside;
fighting to change the system.
They ask too much.

Cultural Dissonance: Job Interviewing and Indigenous Candidates

Sarah Ladd

Abstract

Indigenous Canadians overcome numerous educational barriers before entering the labour market. They encounter yet more barriers at the job search stage, including how to present themselves during job interviews. Since the dominant culture in Canada is individualistic, job seekers from collectivist cultures, including Indigenous populations, are more likely to struggle when framing responses to interview questions to match employer expectations. More qualified Indigenous candidates can be overlooked because they were unable to "sell" themselves due to differences in cultural values.

Recommendations for inclusive hiring and interviewing strategies are explored in response to TRC 7, calling upon the federal government to eliminate employment gaps, and enact TRC 92, which includes a call to ensure that Aboriginal people have access to jobs, training, and education opportunities.

Over a period of 14 years, I have worked at four different western Canadian universities in several career advisor/educator and co-op coordinator roles. Prior to this, I struggled to perform in job interviews, often coming just shy of receiving an offer. After one such failed interview

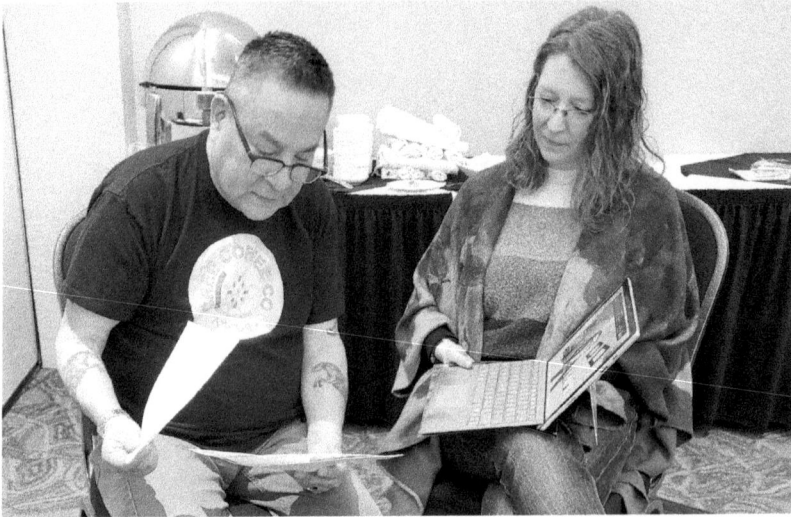

FIGURE 4.1. Sarah Ladd in discussion with Garry Gottfriedson and with Georgann Cope Watson (on screen).
Source: Victoria Handford.

for a promotion in my own department at Simon Fraser University, one of the interviewers invited me to meet with him for some interview coaching. The techniques that he taught were so clear and structured, and made so much sense, that within six months of that meeting I had landed a one-year contract at the University of Calgary as a career advisor and co-op coordinator for the Faculty of Science. I relished the chance to help students find short-term co-op experiences and begin their post-graduation careers. My belief in the interview techniques I had learned was so strong that I shared them enthusiastically with thousands of students there, and later at the University of British Columbia (UBC), with much success. Students routinely contacted me to tell me that they had succeeded using the techniques that I had learned and taught them.

However, after a year or two as a co-op coordinator with the UBC Engineering co-op program, I noticed I was not serving some groups of students well. I routinely struggled with some students from Japan and China when providing career coaching, resume advising, and interview practise. The harder I pushed them to adopt the techniques I taught, the more they withdrew from me. I wanted them to be confident, bold, speak up, and proudly advertise their skills, attributes, and individual accomplishments to potential employers. I did not understand why they could not do this.

To improve, I discussed these struggles with other colleagues, read articles, and attended conference sessions about cultural diversity in career planning and job searching. I started to understand that my teaching framework and content was based in Western corporate culture. This created dissonance for some of the minority group students with whom I worked. A student named Chris, raised in Canada by parents who emigrated from Taiwan, helped me break through to the beginning of an understanding. He and I met several times; I perceived that his introversion was preventing him from succeeding at finding co-op jobs. Chris opened up and shared that he did not feel comfortable talking about himself because he was not raised that way. Our engineering and high-tech sector employers frequently wanted dynamic, high-achieving, strong communicators to join their team. This student described himself as a quiet, modest person who just wanted to work hard and help his team members. Because of this direct cultural mismatch, Chris was unable to connect effectively with employers.

Together, he and I worked out an interview strategy where he could comfortably identify his strengths and explain to employers how he could be a beneficial addition to their team. We adapted some of the Western techniques I taught to better highlight his cultural traits and personal values, in a way that made him feel more comfortable discussing them. I also spoke to some of my employer contacts at companies Chris was interested in, encouraging them to consider characteristics other than those listed in their job descriptions. His first co-op employer rated him as one of the best students they had ever hired, and I could see via a job search website that his career has been a mix of stability and progression, just as he had outlined to me in his long-term career goals and values.

This mutual success left me wanting more; I worked to learn more about intercultural experiences in job searches, and the many employment barriers that immigrants face. For a time, I advised my students to use adapted Western techniques and then encouraged them to work from within companies to change hiring practices as they progressed through their careers. This kind of advice was well-meant but problematic because it puts the responsibility for change on those who are most disadvantaged. I still had much to learn.

Later in my career, I accepted a contract as career advisor/co-op coordinator at Thompson Rivers University. Here I began to provide career advice to a much more diverse student population than I had at UBC, one that included Indigenous students. During the seven years I spent at UBC, I worked with several thousand students but never with one I recognized as, or who self-identified as, Indigenous. On reflection, this is evidence of systemic barriers that prevent Indigenous students from gaining entry to engineering programs in larger schools.

I found myself woefully unprepared to help Indigenous students with the multiple barriers they face in their job search efforts. My time in that role ended before I could learn enough to help Indigenous students. While I no longer work directly with students as a career advisor, in my current administrative role in the Faculty of Education and Social Work (EDSW), I am often involved in staff hiring. This topic is still of great interest and importance to me. When invited to participate in the EDSW decolonization and Indigenization learning journey, I opted to focus my contributions on the employment-related Truth and Reconciliation Commission of Canada Calls to Action 7 and 92 ii.

To explore these two Calls to Action, I will outline the difference between collectivist and individualist cultures, discuss the collectivist nature of many Indigenous cultures, and contrast this with the individualist culture present in the North American corporate sector. From there, I provide an overview of the research into the employment barriers that candidates from collectivist cultures face, followed by information about the specific employment barriers faced by Indigenous people. There is limited research relating to barriers faced by Indigenous Canadians at the job interview stage. Coupled with this, research on Indigenous employment in general is scattered across a multitude of different academic disciplines (Murry & James, 2021), making it difficult to review and interpret relevant literature.

Let me be clear: due to the scope of this work and my lack of a formal research background, I have not conducted research or connected with the local Indigenous community, beyond those Elders, knowledge keepers, and scholars who were invited to collaborate on this collection. My observations, therefore, need to be verified through more extensive discussion with local Secwépemc people, and with other Indigenous populations. I do provide recommendations for future progress toward realizing the Calls to Action 7 and 92 ii, and I offer suggestions that employers and hiring managers may be able to use to begin their own exploration of decolonization and Indigenization of their hiring practices.

Literature Review

Employment barriers for immigrants, particularly those from collectivist cultures, are real and numerous. In my work with international students, I observed that students from some cultures performed better than others in job interviews. I came to understand that the dominant culture in Canada, of which I am part, is an individualist culture, and the students I saw struggle to adapt to North American job interviewing were typically from collectivist cultures. Hofstede (2001) indicates that individualist cultures emphasize an "I" consciousness and their values lean toward individual achievement and initiative, financial security, and the right to privacy, among other traits. Contrastingly, collectivist societies underscore a "we" consciousness. They value collective identity, group solidarity, duties and obligations, and group decision-making. It should be noted that in his work, Hofstede (2001) separated collectivist from individualist cultures along an Eastern versus Western dichotomy but did not include Indigenous cultures in the scope of his work.

In a brief interview, Secwépemc Elder Mike Arnouse (personal communication, April 8, 2022) described his people's world view to me as a pyramid, with two-legged men at the bottom, supporting two-legged women, in turn supporting (in order) plants, water, four-legged animals, and finally reaching the Eagle at the top. The Eagle is an important figure in Secwépemc oral tradition, representing sacred law from above (Connor, 2013). Elder Arnouse shared his understanding that colonial thinking reverses the pyramid, placing men at the pinnacle of the pyramid, with women next, and the natural world below that. He suggested that this wrong thinking leads to man feeling superior and able to dominate others and all of creation, instead of feeling proud to support and care for his family, animals, and the land. This explanation of the Secwépemc world view fits well into the collectivist framework as it emphasizes collective identity, group solidarity, and the importance of duty and obligation.

In her description of her experiences as a graduate student, Viola Cordova wrote, "I say 'we' to indicate my awareness that my view is a result of shared notions" (Cordova & Moore, 2007, p. 158). Cordova also indicates that in her Jicarilla Apache culture, the group surpasses all else, and the sense of "we" dominates the sense of "I." These collectivist themes extend to other Indigenous cultures, which do not have a philosophy of individualism but are oriented instead around family and community and a world view of interrelatedness with others and the environment (McCormick & Amundson, 1997). The need for a model of Indigenous career/life counselling leads me to believe that just as with immigrants from collectivist cultures, a similar dissonance in world view negatively affects Indigenous candidates in their job search. Further, I am concerned that this cultural conflict carries well beyond the job interview, and into the workplace.

The North American workplace is a colonial construct that has evolved from and in a Western, dominant cultural context. The resulting white corporate culture we see today is frequently hierarchical and, though there are some successfully inclusive and diverse workplaces, the majority are characterized by rigidity and intolerance (Murry & James, 2021). This is not limited to the private sector, as hiring in higher education institutions is also fraught with dominant white cultural values, resulting in the exclusion of candidates with culturally diverse backgrounds (Ashlee, 2019).

Other factors inhibit marginalized groups from obtaining long-term work. Current Canadian labour policy and shifts in corporate hiring practices, which originated in the 1990s, have led to increasing numbers of jobs created as short-term contracts with lower risk and cost to employers. This marginalizes those who struggle to enter the labour market. Additionally, government programs, including Employment Insurance, emphasize "work first" and job- and skill-specific training over longer-term career development (MacKinnon, 2015). Both shifts are pushing marginalized individuals and groups further from obtaining long-term career success and stability. I frequently saw this within co-operative education programs, which are designed to give university students learning opportunities. Rather than hiring with the expectation of providing training, companies, as demonstrated by their job descriptions, frequently favoured fourth-year over second-year students. The descriptions had lengthy lists of technical skill requirements. This is becoming a predominant trend in hiring, despite increasing evidence that making up-front investment in training ongoing employees instead of hiring skilled contract employees yields better long-term results and profits (Reilly, 2021).

The inclusion of lists of required skills on job postings, and the interpretation of those skills in interview settings, are culturally embedded in Canadian individualistic norms. When the majority group writes a job description and settles on interview questions, they are inherently biased toward like-minded individuals unless the hiring team undergoes and embraces significant training to identify and combat bias (Ashlee, 2019). The introduction of soft skill requirements that are defined differently from one employer to another polarizes the workforce (Guo, 2015). The Canadian labour market employs rules and principles that advantage those who understand and obey them, and benefit those who create the structures (Bauder, 2005). This includes current interview practices that favour individual achievements and behaviours, such as behavioural-based interviewing (BBI). From my personal and professional experience, I know that BBI questions rely on candidates providing concise and concrete examples of their past actions in a way that displays how their individual contributions, actions, and achievements per task are relevant to the job. I have repeatedly witnessed candidates from cultural backgrounds that value group contributions and collaboration struggle to provide examples that displayed their individual achievements. Even when they were able to do so, many of the students from collectivist cultures reported feeling varying levels of discomfort while pushing themselves to interview in this individualistic style.

Another problematic part of Western hiring practice is the nebulous notion of "fit." The concept of cultural fit in hiring is difficult for some employers to define and sees individual hiring committee members assigning different definitions. The hiring committees for some employers neglect to formally discuss fit and yet it still plays a part in final hiring decisions (Crain & Shepard, 2019). Fit, then, appears to be fluid and open to interpretation and bias from candidate to candidate, and from hiring committee member to hiring committee member. Yet, fit is frequently identified as a critical factor in hiring in North American interviews.

Job interviews may present barriers. Nearly every advertised North American job opportunity requires applicants to go through an interview of some kind. The wealth of information available on interview technique in books, internet articles, and blog posts rarely cites any research on the effectiveness of interviewing. Yet human resource professionals and hiring managers continue to follow essentially the same decades-old job interview formulas despite the lack of evidence indicating that these methods garner the best candidates. Finding research specific to candidates from collectivist cultures is even more difficult.

Immigrants may not be familiar with the conventions of the hiring process in the Canadian labour market, hindering them in successfully navigating job search and interview processes. Often, immigrants are perceived, unconsciously or consciously, to be unlikely to have the cultural competencies needed to succeed in the jobs they are applying to (Bauder, 2005). In fact, applicants from the dominant Western cultural group receive 50 percent more job offers after an interview than their equally qualified visible minority competitors (Quillian et al., 2020).

Because of their collectivist world views, individuals from Indigenous cultures are often perceived by Westerners as being at a lower, more primitive developmental stage in evolution (Cordova & Moore, 2007). This translates to discrimination against those who are not culturally prepared to discuss their accomplishments as individual actions in a job interview. Indigenous collectivist cultural values and sense of self are frequently in direct conflict with white corporate culture (Murry & James, 2021). This cultural clash has the potential to alienate Indigenous candidates before they apply and may also negatively impact a hiring committee's assessment of workplace fit. Dialogue between local Indigenous peoples, government, and corporations to explore this cultural dissonance could be highly beneficial in advancing the Truth and Reconciliation Commission of Canada's Calls to Action 7 and 92.

Before Indigenous job seekers in Canada arrive at the job interview stage, they must overcome numerous complex employment barriers, which may include intergenerational trauma, poverty, addiction, lack of education, geographic location, and restrictive government policies (National Collaborating Centre for Aboriginal Health, 2017). Similarly, educational disadvantage is identified as one of four interconnected aspects affecting Australian Indigenous career seekers; only 5 percent of Indigenous Australians aged 25–29 hold a university degree (Helme, 2010).

Indigenous people who succeed in their educational efforts may face two important additional career barriers: a lack of workplace knowledge and of industry-specific networks. Immigrants who come to Canada with extensive existing professional networks of family and friends fared better in entering the labour market than those who did not (Bauder, 2005) and it is therefore reasonable to assume that Indigenous job seekers lacking networks face similar challenges. Indigenous Australians have limited access to networks of people in paid, professional employment who can assist them in making industry connections (Hunter & Gray, 2006). Without knowledge of workplace and career options, and without access to internal connections in the labour market, Indigenous job seekers are at a distinct disadvantage and must rely on the strength of their application documents alone.

Racism and discrimination stemming from existing and newly developing negative beliefs and stereotypes about Indigenous people have a tremendous adverse impact on Indigenous adult job seekers, and Indigenous youth in school systems. Yet, distressingly, little to no research exists that documents workplace discrimination directed at Indigenous employees and there is a resulting lack of recommendations to guide employers on how to combat this effectively (Murry & James, 2021).

A considerable number of studies identify discrimination against immigrants at the candidate review phase of a job search (whether candidates with ethnic names are less likely to be shortlisted for an interview, for example). However, it is difficult to conduct field experiments to determine the nature and amount of discrimination that may occur between the job interview and job offer stage (Quillian et al., 2020). In one study, fully qualified applicants of visible minorities with cultural attributes that did not fit white corporate norms faced additional disadvantages during job interviews (Quillian et al., 2020). While that study did not focus specifically on discrimination experienced by Indigenous candidates, it makes sense that the divide between Indigenous and Western cultural world views would play the same discriminatory role in the assessment of cultural fit of Indigenous candidates in job interviews.

Recommendations

Change needs to happen in Canada at all levels to improve hiring processes for people in collectivist cultures, including in nation-wide employment policies. In her book, MacKinnon (2015) makes numerous suggestions for decolonizing employment, beginning with federal and provincial labour market policy changes. Her suggestions address the barriers to Indigenous employment from a holistic perspective and would take large-scale shifts to realize. If implemented successfully, her recommendations should result in long-term benefits for Canadian Indigenous people and other marginalized groups.

The suggestions I make here are shorter-term solutions to address immediate problems with the interviewing and hiring stages of employment. They only address those Indigenous job seekers who have already surmounted the numerous other barriers discussed earlier. Both a high-level, long-term nation-wide strategy, and short-term techniques for regional employers, are needed.

The good news is that some organizations in Canada are already working toward truth and reconciliation and are creating programs and policies that support the inclusion of Indigenous peoples in the workplace. Deloitte's *Widening the Circle* (2012) plan emphasizes the importance of putting resources toward Indigenous hiring. It includes numerous recommendations and documents their journey toward dialogue with local Indigenous communities. An additional resource and sign of hope can be found in a list of Canada's 100 Best Diversity Employers, 2022 (Mediacorp Canada Inc., 2022).

Before government and corporate employers can begin to change their hiring, they need to engage in open dialogue with and self-education about local Indigenous cultural ways of knowing and being as a critical first step. When colonial groups choose to identify a problem and then build a solution

without consultation with the group they are attempting to serve, the resulting program or strategy is likely to fail. We need to listen, not advise.

The suggestions I have for employers can be broken into categories:

1. Focus on employee education and community connection;
2. Build hiring committees with diversity and inclusivity in mind;
3. Develop interview processes that do not disadvantage those with
   collectivist world views; and
4. Actively challenge racism and discrimination in the hiring
   process.

Employee Education and Community Connection

Employers and hiring managers must start by recognizing that no one
practice or policy will work for all Indigenous cultures, just as no single inclusive hiring policy will work for every cultural group globally.
Provide educational opportunities for your employees to learn more
about local Indigenous culture, and, importantly, provide connection
points. Take your employees into the local communities as part of that
education process.

A critical next step is to learn about the culture and world views of
each local Indigenous population through direct consultation, and then
to collaborate when welcomed by the Indigenous community, as per their
protocols, before developing inclusive hiring processes. For example, one
study showed that Australian Indigenous career seekers wished to find jobs
that make a difference to their community (Helme, 2010). The information
in this study was gathered directly from Elders and community members.
This practice can be easily repeated through communication and connection with local Canadian Indigenous communities.

Companies seeking Indigenous employees may wish to invest time
and resources in building personal relationships with those in their local
Indigenous communities and to provide mentorship opportunities and
networking connections for job seekers. This may be best achieved by
visiting local Indigenous communities, first seeking invitation to do so.
In the Torres Strait region of Australia, researchers found that connecting with Elders helped to foster understanding of Western medicine and
health, which in turn led to increased interest from Indigenous candidates
for positions in the health care system (Bailey et al., 2021).

Inclusive Hiring Committees

Effort should be made to include Indigenous employees in hiring committees whenever possible; a highly diverse committee with other visible minorities represented should be the goal. There is a caveat here. We need to be aware that we are placing a burden on Indigenous and minority group employees beyond their regular job duties in asking them to individually represent their entire cultural group and act as a voice for other cultures (Deloitte, 2012). Where possible, it would be wise to consider hiring Indigenous consultants to shoulder some of this burden, either as contractors or to create new positions within organizations dedicated to this work. A labour market intermediary (LMI) for Indigenous career seekers could offer a holistic approach to individually address barriers prior to, during, and after entry to the labour market (MacKinnon 2015). Employers interested in hiring Indigenous candidates could partner with local organizations, Indigenous groups, and/or post-secondary institutions to hire LMIs to provide this service.

Interview Processes

Changes could be made to interview questions so they reflect strengths-based hiring practices and seek people with potential, rather than only candidates who meet requirements on lists of skills, criminal record checks, and so on (Bailey et al., 2021). When writing interview questions, it is possible to add some that focus on group effort/achievements and bring to light how a candidate works in a team, rather than solely seeking out examples and answers that demonstrate individual achievement.

Because Indigenous people often see their own views as having little separation from the views of their community (Cordova & Moore, 2007), they may struggle to express their strengths and attributes in an interview setting. Consider conducting reference checks earlier, and/or encourage the inclusion of Elders, knowledge keepers, and other key community members as character references in lieu of professional references (where needed). Elder Mike Arnouse shared with me that in his community, Elders have deep love for and knowledge of the members of their community and are well-situated to speak about their abilities (personal communication, April 7, 2022).

Racism and Discrimination

Finally, recognizing and confronting colonial hiring practices by identifying biases is essential to making progress (Ashlee, 2019). Examining the hiring process, from the job posting language to the hiring committee composition to the definition of "fit," will help organizations make progress toward dismantling racist hiring practices. I recognize that this is a major undertaking, and likely requires considerable ongoing commitment from each employer or government organization, equity, diversity, and inclusion committees, and dedicated personnel and financial resources. However, investment in dismantling racism and discrimination will benefit not only Indigenous job seekers, but aids all those who face discrimination: visible minorities, differently abled persons, LGBTQ2S+, and women.

Conclusion

My memories of working with Chris, the student whose parents were from Taiwan, have not faded and though I am proud of what he and I achieved together, I recognize the many other ways that I could have better served him and, later, Indigenous students. We all have these formative moments in our careers and personal lives, and it is important that we hold onto them to motivate ourselves to continued growth. I have a long way to go in my work toward understanding and then participating in decolonization, truth, and reconciliation. I must be patient but persistent with myself, as I observe colonial behaviours and actions in my professional and personal life. First, I must observe, then I must act.

Continuing to listen to what Indigenous Canadians are telling us is important, especially when it is hard to hear, as it can be for those of us who, like me, are descended from those who directly harmed Indigenous people. Following a speech by one of our Secwépemc Elders that included information I was struggling to come to terms with, former Associate Dean Dr. Jane Hewes advised me that we need to hear the uncomfortable truths, and that being uncomfortable is important and often necessary.

The TRC's Calls to Action related to Indigenous employment in Canada are incredibly important. When employment barriers are diminished, larger numbers of Indigenous Canadians will be able enter the workforce and have meaningful and rewarding careers that meet their needs and match their cultural values. This, in turn, will affect further positive change. Senior leaders in government, public institutions, and private corporations can develop larger-scale policies for long-term change. Hiring managers and administrators like me can ensure there are Indigenous voices on hiring committees and can set in place practices that create more interviews that do not disadvantage Indigenous and collectivist cultures.

Working toward truth and reconciliation will take time, and it will take thousands upon thousands of people, each taking small and large actions.

References

Ashlee, K. C. (2019). You'll fit right in: Fit as a euphemism for whiteness in higher education hiring practices. In Reece, B. J., Tran, V. T., Devore, E. N., and Porcaro, G. (Eds.), *Debunking the myth of job fit in higher education and student affairs* (pp. 49–66). Stylus Publishing.

Bailey, J., Blignault, I., Renata, P., Naden, P., Nathan, S., & Newman, J. (2021). Barriers and enablers to Aboriginal and Torres Strait islander careers in health: A qualitative, multisector study in western New South Wales. *Australian Journal of Rural Health*, 29, 897–909. https://doi.org/10.1111/ajr.12764

Bauder, H. (2005). Habitus, rules of the labour market and employment strategies of immigrants in Vancouver, Canada. *Social and Cultural Geography*, 6(1), 81–97. https://www.tandfonline.com/doi/full/10.1080/1464936052000335982

Brewer, M. B., & Chen, Y.-R. (2007). Where (who) are collectives in collectivism? Toward conceptual clarification of individualism and collectivism. *Psychological Review*, 114(1), 133–151. https://doi.org/10.1037/0033-295X.114.1.133

Connor, K. (2013). *Tribal Case Book—Secwépemc Stories and Legal Traditions.* [Stsmémelt Project Tek'wémiple7 Research]. https://secwepemcstrong.com/wp-content/uploads/2021/02/Tribal-Case-Book.pdf

Cordova, V. F., & Moore, K. D. (2007). *How it is: The Native American philosophy of V.F. Cordova.* University of Arizona Press.

Crain, L. K., and Shepard, M. J. L. (2019). Employer definitions of and reflections on fit in hiring processes. In Reece, B. J., Tran, V. T., Devore, E. N., and Porcaro, G. (Eds.), *Debunking the myth of job fit in higher education and student affairs* (pp. 49–66). Stylus Publishing.

Deloitte. (2012). *Widening the circle: Increasing opportunities for Aboriginal people in the workplace.* https://www2.deloitte.com/content/dam/Deloitte/ca/Documents/about-deloitte/ca-en-about-deloitte-widening-the-circle.pdf

Guo, S. (2015). The colour of skill: Contesting a racialised regime of skill from the experience of recent immigrants in Canada. *Studies in Continuing Education*, 37(3), 236–250. https://doi.org/10.1002/j.2161-1920.1997.tb00467.x

Helme, S. (2010). Career decision-making: What matters to Indigenous Australians? *Australian Journal of Career Development (ACER Press)*, 19(3), 67–74. https://doi.org/10.1177/103841621001900309

Hofstede, G. H. (2001). *Culture's consequences: Comparing values, behaviors, institutions, and organizations across nations* (2nd ed.). Sage Publications.

Hunter, B. H., & Gray, M. C. (2006). The Effectiveness of Indigenous job search strategies. *Economic Record*, 82(256), 1–10. https://doi.org/10.1111/j.1475-4932.2006.00289.x

MacKinnon, S. (2015). *Decolonizing employment: Aboriginal inclusion in Canada's labour market.* University of Manitoba Press.

McCormick, R. M., & Amundson, N. E. (1997). A career-life planning model for First Nations people. *Journal of Employment Counseling, 34*(4), 171–179. https://doi.org/10.1002/j.2161-1920.1997.tb00467.x

Mediacorp Canada Inc. (2022). *Canada's best 100 diversity employers (2022): Winners from our 15th annual editorial competition.* https://www.canadastop100.com/diversity/

Murry, A. T., & James, K. (2021). Reconciliation and industrial–organizational psychology in Canada. *Canadian Journal of Behavioural Science / Revue Canadienne Des Sciences Du Comportement, 53*(2), 114–124. https://doi.org/10.1037/cbs0000237

National Collaborating Centre for Aboriginal Health. (2017). *Employment as a social determinant of First Nations, Inuit and Métis health.* https://www.ccnsa-nccah.ca/docs/determinants/FS-Employment-SDOH-2017-EN.pdf

Reilly, K. (2021, November 1). LinkedIn's COO on Why New Hires Shouldn't "Hit the Ground Running." [Blog post]. https://www.linkedin.com/business/talent/blog/talent-strategy/why-new-hires-should-not-hit-the-ground-running

Quillian, L., Lee, J. J., and Oliver, M. (2020). Evidence from field experiments in hiring shows substantial additional racial discrimination after the callback. *Social Forces, 99*(2), 732–759.

COMMEMORATION CALLS TO ACTION

The Truth and Reconciliation Commission (2015, p. 9) made five Calls to Action in relation to commemoration. Issues named as priorities for changes in relation to commemoration are:

79. We call upon the federal government, in collaboration with Survivors, Aboriginal organizations, and the arts community, to develop a reconciliation framework for Canadian heritage and commemoration. This would include, but not be limited to:
    i. Amending the Historic Sites and Monuments Act to include First Nations, Inuit, and Métis representation on the Historic Sites and Monuments Board of Canada and its Secretariat.
    ii. Revising the policies, criteria, and practices of the National Program of Historical Commemoration to integrate Indigenous history, heritage values, and memory practices into Canada's national heritage and history.
    iii. Developing and implementing a national heritage plan and strategy for commemorating residential school sites, the history and legacy of residential schools, and the contributions of Aboriginal peoples to Canada's history.
80. We call upon the federal government, in collaboration with Aboriginal peoples, to establish, as a statutory holiday,

a National Day for Truth and Reconciliation to honour
Survivors, their families, and communities, and ensure
the public commemoration of the history and legacy
of residential schools remains a vital component of the
reconciliation process.

81. We call upon the federal government, in collaboration with
Survivors and their organizations, and other parties to the
Settlement Agreement, to commission and install a publicly
accessible, highly visible Residential Schools National
Monument in the city of Ottawa to honour Survivors
and all the children who were lost to their families and
communities.

82. We call upon provincial and territorial governments, in
collaboration with Survivors and their organizations, and
other parties to the Settlement Agreement, to commission
and install a publicly accessible, highly visible Residential
Schools Monument in each capital city to honour Survivors
and all the children who were lost to their families and
communities.

83. We call upon the Canada Council for the Arts to establish,
as a funding priority, a strategy for Indigenous and non-
Indigenous artists to undertake collaborative projects and
produce works that contribute to the reconciliation process.

References

Truth and Reconciliation Commission of Canada. (2015). *Truth and Reconciliation
Commission of Canada: Calls to Action.* https://ehprnh2mwo3.exactdn.com/wp-
content/uploads/2021/01/Calls_to_Action_English2.pdf

An Unholy Act

Garry Gottfriedson

cutting off fingers
stealing for starving
kids imprisoned
might satisfy cruel
catholic intentions

slicing skin and bone
a blade at a time
to show example
and offer penance
is an unholy act
regardless

contrition and sacrament
does not erase
wrongdoings
no matter how close
you are to god

shame and guilt
kills anything good
believing in hope
brings peace of mind

but what good does
it do on empty bellies
and forever reminders
like missing fingers?

Debwewin[*]

Victoria Handford

Sometimes truth touches with whispering wind in long grasses or
      tinkling of the ziibaaska'igan dancers.
Sometimes truth embraces when a bird clutching salmon
      agilely ascends, lands on its nest, and feeds eaglets.
Sometimes truth caresses, we are sad, a friend strokes our shoulder,
      touch brushing with comfort and energy.
Sometimes truth nudges, smells of baking bread,
      fragrant hints of histories – and herstories.
Sometimes truth holds us when family and community gather;
     rejoicing and celebrating the
      love of hundreds of generations of caring.
Sometimes – when truth is complete, truth changes who we are.
     This deep, heartfelt, complete truth is Debwewin.
Debwewin is not easy or comfortable, but
     carries embers igniting healing.

---

[*]   This poem and the story that follows were written following many hours of conversation with Peter Edwards, author and reporter with the *Toronto Star*. Peter wrote many articles about the Ipperwash crisis. His relationship with Sam George, brother of Dudley George who was killed by an Ontario Provincial Police sniper, was essential to Peter's telling of the story in his 2003 book *One Dead Indian: The Premier, the Police, and the Ipperwash Crisis* (McClelland & Stewart).

Sam wanted to know the whole truth. All of it. Debwewin.

This story happened when Sam was young. Think how old Mother Nature is! Think how old some of our community Elders are! Sam was young. His search for truth was a quest only the young are willing to go on. In the grand scheme of things, Sam was just a little older than you are.

Sam grew up on the Kettle and Stony Point First Nation Reserve. It was a beautiful place, with sand and long grasses, tall cornstalks, smooth rocks, and the big Lake Huron. Lake Huron is huge. It is like an ocean!*

Before Sam was born, Canada decided it needed to go to war. And many of Sam's family went overseas and fought in that terrible war. The government decided to borrow some of the land that belonged to the Chippewa and Stony Point Nations for a training site for soldiers.

When the war was over the community found the government had used their ancient burial grounds as a munitions dump. The community was mad.

There was another problem.

The people of Kettle and Stony Point said, "While our men were away fighting for Canada, the government took away some of our lands—the Stony Point lands of Ipperwash. The government said they needed it as a place to train soldiers. But after the war was over, the government did not give the land back."

The people outside the Kettle and Stony Point Nation said "So what? We all get to use this beautiful park. We need places to be on the land as well. We like vacationing here. The government should not give the land back."

The government and the Nation argued back and forth.

Many governments came and went. All of them just wanted to be re-elected. So, nothing changed.

Dudley George, Sam's brother, got more and more frustrated. He started protesting many of the actions that were oppressing Aboriginal people in Canada and his family on the Stoney Point Reserve.**

---

* This is a children's story. If this story were published as a children's book it would need multiple illustrations that both support and engage the reader.

** The Kettle and Stony Point Reserve and the Stoney Point Reserve are two different reserves. There are many family connections between the two, it is often confusing for people. A chapter in the Report of the *Ipperwash Inquiry—Volume 1*, provides significant historical context that is useful.

But government is government. It holds all the cards. Dudley was seen as "a crazy Indian," "a nuisance Indian." He was a pain in the neck of government. Nothing changed.

The Stoney Point people got more restless. They had been arguing and losing, arguing, and losing—for 50 years. There were meetings about what to do.

"We should take over the park," said Dudley. "We should simply take our land back. It is our land. We will just move into the park and stay there. They will give it back if we don't give up."

Not everyone agreed this was a good idea. There was lots of discussion.

"What if the government takes away more of our land?" asked one person.

"What if the government takes away our sports arena?" asked another.

"What if the government says we are just problem Indians?" said many.

They decided the government could not make things any worse. The government already said all Indians were problems. There was nothing to lose! But it still took a long time for the community to reach agreement on a plan. Dudley and Sam were part of the planning, of course. Sam worried about Dudley, whose intensity was great—but risky. Dudley wanted change now. Sam believed change would take seven generations. Sam was not only patient—he was steadfast.

Both approaches appeared in the plans—the steadfast plan and the impatient plan. There were shifts of protesters, plans for food, and plans to replan as things went along. There were stages of protest—first a few people, then a few more. Sam was still a bit uneasy about Dudley's impatience.

Sam said, "Well, okay Dudley. But let us make this about community-building, not just anger building."

Dudley responded, "Okay Sam. I agree. That is what we do when we stand up for ourselves. We are stronger than we realize. When we protest our muscles grow."

The protests at Ipperwash Provincial Park started. The Stony Point people protested for many days and weeks.

The public wanted their camping spots along the shores of the lake back!

"I reserved that camping spot—I have a right to go," said one.

"I have gone on this weekend to Ipperwash for 30 years. I have a right to go," said another.

"I want to have a party with my friends," said one high school graduate. "I have a right to go."

The local newspaper supported the public. There was no explanation of the history, or of the generosity of the Stony Point people for 50 years, in the paper. It was all about getting the park back.

Things got worse. There was more anger.

The newspaper editor said, "We'll come back and tell the story when they figure this out." And they walked away.

There are always people like this—they do not understand that the land was never theirs.

The anger grew. The police were tired. The Stony Point people were tired. The public was tired. The government in Toronto was tired. Dark storm clouds continued to form—something was going to happen.

One night, after the park was closed, when the protesters were cooking and settling into their camps for the night, the police arrived at the park with assault rifles. An assault rifle shoots 600 bullets-a-minute.

The police walked into the quiet, closed, dark park and confronted the protesters. The Stony Point people had no weapons. They had their pots and pans, their tents, and their principles.

"Get out of our park," called the police over the loudspeaker. "You cannot stay here."

Dudley George replied, "This is not your park. This is our land. We want it back."

The police opened fire.

Dudley was dead—just like that.

The next day, Peter, a young man from Toronto, arrived. Peter worked for a very large national newspaper. He was there to "get the story" for the newspaper.

Peter had grown up in Lytton, British Columbia, a town with about 800 people, 600 of whom were from six different First Nation communities. Peter's dad, the town doctor, had ended the segregation practice of having Aboriginal people enter the hospital through a separate door. Yup, Canada has its own stories of segregation. Canada has its own Rosa Parks, its own stories of apartheid.* But they are not known.

---

* The story of Rosa Parks was one of the sparks that ignited the civil rights movement in the United States. She refused to give up her seat to a white man (see https://www.youtube.com/watch?v=aCcSsjkQe9s).

Peter met Sam in a restaurant to "get the story." Sam brought hundreds of family pictures, filled with people smiling, enjoying their times together.

This was not what usually happened at Peter's stories of crime. Sam's soft voice was almost a whisper, likely a result of the shock of his brother's death.

"I need the truth," Sam said quietly.

Peter asked him to explain what this, saying "What do you mean—the truth?"

Sam repeated, just as softly: "I need the truth."

There was quiet between Sam and Peter.

Later, Peter met with Elder Tommy White. Tommy explained "truth" to Peter, saying, "The word *truth* is the way of saying this in English. But the word in our language is *Debwewin*. It means to know the facts, have all the facts correct. And to have healing in the heart that comes from the facts being known to be true."

Peter felt Tommy had said what the exact purpose of a reporter was. He said, "If my job doesn't mean I get to the truth then what is the point in doing the job?"

Peter kept talking to people.

The police story was complicated—there was something not being told. It began to feel like the story was being covered up.

One friend of Peter's, feeling frustrated that the story would not go away, and annoyed that Peter was so invested in the story, yelled at him, "Come on, move on. The decision was made to confront them. It's one dead Indian."

Peter did not flinch. Peter dug in.

While Peter worked on the story, Sam started mobilizing people. He did many speaking engagements in schools and universities, at community meetings—wherever anyone asked him to speak Sam went.

One person said to Sam, "You know, I spoke 17 times this month, I'm so tired."

Sam replied, "Yeah, I know. I did 31 speeches this month. And slept in my car as I drove across the province to do them. It can be tiring." Sam worked hard. He knew justice would work if he made it work—and only if he made it work.

Sam's "truthmobile" travelled back and forth across the province. Sam invited many people, of all ages, races, genders, and incomes to help find the truth in the situation. Sam worked with many Indigenous lawyers who helped to make the system work. Sam worked with many children and students who helped to make the system work. And Sam worked with his community, and other Indigenous communities, to help to make the system work. And...

Some people started saying, "What would Sam do?" And they did it! Sam knew that to get the whole truth he needed these allies. He knew that many little steps were needed by many people to get to the truth.

Some people became allies with Sam. Sam found ways to make everyone feel valued, important, and part of the community of action.

It worked.

It took many years. Truth takes time. The goal was to "look into and report on events surrounding the death of Dudley George and to make recommendations focused on the avoidance of violence in similar circumstances" (see Chiefs of Ontario, 2012).

Sam got the truth. It took years and years of hard work. Sam used his grief to get the truth. He used his sense of humour, while working with hundreds of people, including allies from many cultural backgrounds, to get the truth.

The truth did speak to the heart. And Sam knew he had made a difference.

Sam was given the Order of Ontario in 2007. It was a nice gesture. Not that Sam ever did any of this for an award.

Peter was given an eagle feather by the Union of Ontario Indians and a medal from the Centre for Human Rights. Not that Peter ever did any of this for awards.

For Dudley, for Sam, for the Chippewas of Kettle and Stony Point Nation, for Peter and the many allies, there was a full truth.

Debwewin.

But.

The land of Ipperwash was returned, in 2016, to the Chippewas of Kettle and Stony Point.

The rustle of the wind whispers: "There is more truth to tell."

The animals chatter: "There is more truth to tell."

The smell of the baking bread reminds us: "There is more truth to tell."

The community joins together and, in the dancing, the storytelling, the friendship—everyone knows: "There is more truth to tell."

There is more truth to tell.

References

Chiefs of Ontario. (2012, May 31). *First Nations in Ontario question provincial government commitment on the fifth anniversary of the Ipperwash Inquiry Report* [Press release]. https://www.newswire.ca/news-releases/first-nations-in-ontario-question-provincial-government-commitment-on-the-fifth-anniversary-of-ipperwash-inquiry-report-510307691.html

Red Bridge

Victoria Handford

Abstract

Monuments tell stories that are often representative of the dominant history. This chapter considers Red Bridge, a transportation link in Kamloops, and a historic, local monument of progress. I consider both the official stories and other possible issues related to Red Bridge. "Those in power write the history, while those who suffer write the songs" (Harte, as cited in Moloney, 2005). This bridge has a history recorded in many locations. It also has songs of suffering. Truth is a complicated discovery—this chapter considers possible nuances of history.

The Truth and Reconciliation Commission's Calls to Action were released in 2015. By 2017 I was quite familiar with this document. That same year a kiosk celebrating a local heritage site, Red Bridge, was built. It may have been that its opening, while the Calls to Action were beginning to take shape in my mind and heart, caused me to read its historic plaques many times and reflect on the told history of the bridge. Was it true that Red Bridge received its name because the structure, as local lore reported, had originally had a red hue in the wood? This essay examines this question.

When I was a little girl, I was crossing the street, holding my father's hand. I saw something in the distance and asked him questions that went something like this:

"Daddy, why are those men gathered by that statue?"
He responded
"They are there because it is Remembrance Day, and they are
    remembering the war."
Full of questions, I asked
"What war were they in?"
Dad answered
"Most of them were in World War I or II."
I asked the obvious question:
"Why aren't you over there? You were in World War II."
There was a long, long pause. Finally, he said
"Remembrance Day is more about creating a will to go to war. It is
    telling the preferred story of war, one of brave people, one of heroes.
    That story is not what I lived. War is not something to celebrate."

I have never forgotten the stillness of my father as he answered me. I knew to ask no more questions—ever.

Many years later, I gave my father a book written by a friend of his titled *And No Birds Sang*. The author, Farley Mowat, happened to serve in Italy in World War Two with my dad. My father read that book at least four times. He never ever talked about it, but it clearly "spoke" to my father's truth. He never recovered from the trauma of war—but received healing in seeing the truth told.

A Little about Kamloops

After living in a variety of locations in Ontario and in other countries, I moved to Kamloops, British Columbia, a city of about 90,000 people, about 10 years ago. I have had the opportunity to learn about Kamloops from the perspective of an "outsider."

From my office window I can see long river valleys between mountains. Kamloops is located at the confluence of the North and South Thompson Rivers. These rivers exist because they are draining the watersheds of the nearby high mountains of the Rockies, the Selkirks, and other mountain ranges in the area. The Thompson River system is a major waterway in the interior of British Columbia. In late spring and summer, the river waters are full to overflowing. From late summer until spring, the river flow is low. I sometimes imagine how people crossed the rivers at the bottoms of these valleys in days gone by. Most often when I look at the rivers, I ponder how the valleys will look as glaciers melt and there is minimal water to supply these rivers. Global warming is going to be difficult for all of us. A topic for a different essay.

The two rivers are natural division points in Kamloops; these major barriers or arteries split the current city into distinct "neighbourhoods." Early in my time in Kamloops I found travelling to places in and beyond the city involved taking one of the four bridges across these rivers, arriving in areas that were distinct and separate from each other.

Soon I was being directed to use a grey-coloured bridge called Red Bridge to cross the South Thompson River as the larger bridge to the west was under construction. The first few times I used Red Bridge I was amazed that it still existed. It is a significant structure yet was built of wood and consisted of two narrow lanes for vehicle traffic and a narrow pedestrian sidewalk. It unites the south side of the river, the downtown area of Kamloops, and a mostly industrial subdivision on the north side of the river, a part of the Tk'emlúps Reserve. Both areas seemed fully served by two other multi-lane bridges, one on either side of Red Bridge. I concluded that the bridge was likely of historical importance and accepted that as its main purpose. It was useful during bridge repairs, but otherwise felt like a secondary route across the river.

As a newcomer, I was also a bit confused about the name of the bridge. I kept asking myself: Why is this grey bridge called Red Bridge? When I asked long-time residents of Kamloops, their answers can be summarized as, "It's always been called this, that's why." This is the way communities often are—they evolve, and most of the population does not know or remember why something is the way it is, they just accept what they've been told. Still curious, I did a search for bridges of Kamloops, and found a website (Stainton, n.d.), which identified and told historical tales about a number of bridges, but, oddly, did not feature Red Bridge.

My question gradually drifted into the background, only to be revived in 2017, when a kiosk with plaques recounting the story of Red Bridge was placed in Pioneer Park, on the south side of the South Thompson River. I remember being so pleased because now I would get answers! I read the information carefully.

The Kiosks

There are two kiosks that provide histories of the bridge. They are very similar to each other, and in many parts are identical. I will focus on the kiosk in Pioneer Park (ironically, this is situated on the site of a former settlement community for the Secwépemc, but that is another story), but pictures of both kiosks are below. The smaller kiosk is figure 13.1, the larger kiosk and the one in Pioneer Park is figure 13.2.

Each side of the park's kiosk displays information about the history of the bridge. The red roof and red paint on the kiosk reinforce that red is important as a colour and is the bridge's name. Heritage Canada was one important financial supporter for the kiosk. Other significant donors are named on each side of the kiosk or in brickwork surrounding the kiosk.

The benches, one on each of the four sides of the kiosk, also memorialize individuals identified in the kiosk display. These benches are a natural spot for people to step off the walking trail and have a rest. It is quite common to see people pausing to read the kiosk panels.

The accounts on four sides of the kiosks focus on: the origin story, the first bridge, the second and third bridge, and donors.

The Origin Story

This side of the kiosk describes the history of the Tk'emlúps te Secwépemc Band prior to the establishment of the first fur trading post in 1812. It identifies these original peoples as hunter/gatherers who lived on the land in summers and in *keekwillie*, or pit houses, on the shores of the South Thompson River in winter. The origin story also describes a hazardous ferry system that existed prior to the construction of the bridge. This ferry was dangerous because of the size of the river, the current, and the ice in spring, fall, and winter. The ferry system did not work well for settlers who were moving crops and livestock from one side of the river to the other and they successfully lobbied for funding for a bridge. Hli-hleh-Kan, whose English name is Chief Louis, is identified as important to the Tk'emlúps Nation as they worked with settlers over several decades around the time of building Red Bridge.

The First Bridge

In government documents this was called "Government Bridge." Built in 1887, it stood from 1887 until 1912. The detailed information on the kiosk includes items such as financing, height, construction (suspension, swing), and that it took two months to build the bridge. Dan Adams won the government contract to build the bridge. It states the bridge became known by locals as Red Bridge because of the red hue of the Douglas fir beams.

FIGURE 5.1. Red Bridge marker and historical kiosk.
Source: Victoria Handford.

FIGURE 5.2. Red Bridge kiosk in Pioneer Park with the bridge in the background.
Source: Victoria Handford.

The Second and Third Bridge

These two sides of the kiosk describe the second and third rebuilds of Red Bridge and include historic pictures of paddlewheelers travelling the river, women on horseback, and the wood of the bridge itself. The resources transported by water as well as the water routes themselves are identified. A fire destroyed the second bridge in 1931 and a new one was built in 1936. Side panels provide some history of Howe trusses, and how the piers were sheeted in planking with triangular, ice-breaking corners. The information identifies enhancements to the current bridge made when establishing it as a historic site. When the larger Yellowhead Bridge was built to the east in 1968, there was some talk of dismantling Red Bridge. The railing on the walkway along the bridge was painted fire-engine red in 1970, a request made by the Downtown Business Association.

Donors

The fourth side of the kiosk includes dedications, memorials, and the names of people who contributed financially to the kiosk development and construction.

The kiosk answered some of my questions. This bridge was granted historic site status by Heritage Canada. My main question remained, particularly because the red railing had been added and dutifully maintained for some reason but was jarring on this historic bridge. The bridge was not red. So, I kept looking for answers to why the structure was called Red Bridge.

Online Information

When I searched for online information using the terms "Red Bridge," "Kamloops," and "History," several images, news stories, and other pieces of information surfaced. I reviewed the first 12 pages of this search and identified three information sources related to the history of the bridge, which seemed credible.

Frontier to Freeway: A Short, Illustrated History of the Roads in British Columbia

This document was published by the Ministry of Transportation and Highways of British Columbia in 1986, the year construction began on the Coquihalla Highway, an ambitious and important highway project in British Columbia. It outlines seven phases of transportation development, each representing an era of travel. It also provides a history of ferry transportation and how difficult transportation development was in the very challenging—and beautiful—province of British Columbia.

The seven phases of transportation development identified are: First Nations Trails, Fur Trails (1805), Gold Trails (1840s), Wagon Roads (1860s), Trunk Roads (1873), Modern Engineered Highways (first half of the twentieth century), and Multi-Lane Highways (second half of the twentieth century). It was during the Trunk Road era that Government Bridge was built (1887), a phase of the building of bridges and roads intended to enable movement and settlement. This construction created a network of transportation that united the newly formed country of Canada and aided in settlement by farmers and ranchers who were immigrating to the interior of British Columbia. Government Bridge was part of this initiative.

Kamloops Heritage Commission

The Kamloops Heritage Commission website identifies "the Kamloops Red Bridge as being significant for historical, cultural and economic values." The website provides a succinct history of the bridge and its iterations, beginning the history with the building of the bridge in 1887. It identifies the importance of the bridge to the Tk'emlúps Indian Band Reserve and pioneer farming and ranching settlement. It speaks about the bridge being a link between two cultures, the Tk'emlúps Indian Band on the north shore of the South Thompson River and the predominately white population of the city on the south shore. A short history of the Tk'emlúps Indian Band of the Secwépemc Nation is provided.

Western Canadian Heritage

The Western Canadian Heritage website states:

> This old wood timber truss bridge has been known as the Red Bridge for some time, as, though it can't be seen from this vantage point, much of it has been painted red since anyone can remember. The bridge itself is older than anyone can remember. (Western Canadian Heritage)

The original bridge was known to have been built using Douglas fir, a wood known for its durability and strength. While not noted on this website, Douglas fir is known to be a hard wood that is resistant to abrasion. It is reportedly a good product for building wharves, trestles, bridge parts, log homes, and commercial buildings.

According to the website, the bridge, in its several iterations, reflects local transportation history, at least from "the era of horse and wagon transport to automobile traffic." The history does mention the hunter-gatherer as well as nomadic history of Tk'emlúps Indian Band and Secwépemc Nation, sharing that pit houses, sometimes known as keekwillie houses, burial sites, and artifacts can be viewed at the Secwépemc Museum and Heritage Park.

Finally, the website provides a list of "character"-defining elements in relation to the bridge, including:

> The bridge is centrally located and provides views of Mount Paul, Mount Peter and the conjunction of South Thompson and North Thompson Rivers. From the sidewalk deck, views of the federal designated heritage Canadian National Railway station built in 1927, Riverside Park established in 1905, the Indian Residential School opened in 1890 and Pioneer Park all contribute to its heritage character.

The above quote also appears on the Kamloops Heritage Commission website. It is a beautiful structure. The Western Canadian Heritage website notes that the bridge was accorded heritage status in 2007.

The bridge has historic significance for the region and for British Columbia, both architecturally and culturally. The bridge was built as part of the trunk roads initiative. It increased the safety of crossing the fast-moving, powerful South Thompson River, particularly during the three months of spring run-off and freeze-up. The bridge would have saved many lives over the years.

The building of the bridge made transporting crops and other goods easier. When trips to market become easier, settlement often is more rapid and population growth larger.

Some issues exist in the information provided on the kiosk, the publication, and websites. Given the bridge was built in 1887 within the eras of careful government records, it is likely an exaggeration to say that it is "older than anyone can remember." While no one is living who remembers this bridge being constructed, people had likely heard about it through intergenerational stories.

The Western Canadian Heritage website identifies it was originally built in 1887 and named the Government Bridge but was colloquially known as Red Bridge because of the red hue of the wood. When the bridge was rebuilt in 1912 and again in 1936 it may have had red hues if Douglas fir was used (unknown), but today the bridge does not look at all red to me. Despite the research, I still was not committing to this popular version of the history of Red Bridge. It felt sanitized.

Colours and the Bridges of Kamloops

Colour of Bridges

Information found on a website called The Shore (Stainton, n.d.) indicates that residents used colours to identify bridges. The website begins the bridge stories of Kamloops with the Thompson River Bridge (locally called "White Bridge"), which was built in the early 1900s (some evidence suggests 1901, however the BC *Sessional Papers* suggest it was 1904), about three kilometres to the west of Red Bridge. According to the *Sessional Papers*, the bridge was unpainted. No money was allocated to paint the bridge. It was following the building of the bridge that it was painted white, hence its colloquial name. The White Bridge was condemned in 1923.

This website identifies a third Thompson River bridge known as "Black Bridge" (1925–1961), which was constructed just east of the former White Bridge. A fourth bridge, locally known as "Blue Bridge" (officially named the Overlanders Bridge), whose steel undergirding was painted blue, was built in 1961. The Halston Bridge was built in 1984, which seems to have had no colour name.

Beyond these bridges, a Canadian National Railway (CNR) bridge was constructed in 1914. This bridge was part of the rail line connecting Edmonton, Alberta, to Kamloops. This bridge, which is black in colour, is the oldest existing original bridge in Kamloops.

In summary, Kamloops has had, in its history, four bridges named by unofficially by colour (red, white, black, and blue), one bridge named Halston, and one known as the CNR bridge. So, how did this decision to name bridges by colours get started? It seemed to me it all began with Red Bridge. So, the name Red Bridge needs further consideration.

Hues of Wood

I shifted my research to investigate the colour of the wood. If it was called Red Bridge for the last 150 years because of the colour of the wood in 1887, surely the wood had to have remained red for a long time, despite its evident grey nature today (sans red-painted railing). I contacted the Ministry of Natural Resources and asked: "How long (in years, approximately) would we imagine it would take for Douglas fir to turn from its reddish/brown colour to a grey colour when it is sitting in the Thompson River?"

The first response was: "Doug fir would turn in the [N]orth Thompson in a month, in the [S]outh Thompson as the water is clearer; maybe six months? Ish" (J. McGrath, personal communication, March 1, 2022).

Following up, I asked, "Would that include the parts of the bridge that are not sitting directly in the water?"

The response was: "This depends on the amount of sun, the colour changes on green cut timbers fast" (March 2, 2022).

Then I wondered about the possible impact of any treatment of the wood. If it had been treated, would it have helped the bridge retain its red hue? The response was that while treating the wood helps Douglas fir retain its red/brown hues, "even treated fir will begin to gray after a few years." And it was not common practice to treat wood in 1887. The British Columbia *Sessional Papers* do not indicate "painting" of the wood or treating the wood in the costs for building the bridge. Just to be sure, the detailed costs for painting the bridge were not simply so small they were not included in the *Sessional Papers*; I reviewed the details for the Harrison River Hot Springs Ditch Road and found the *Sessional Papers* for this identified the contract for the ditch was awarded to Jas. McDonald for a total of $1.00. Another example found in the same sessional paper was the awarding of a contract for tarring cylinders for the Point Ellice Bridge. The award to John Morris was for $25.00. (British Columbia, 1887, pp. 312, 309). Small amounts of money were all described and accounted for in the *Sessional Papers*. It can be assumed there was no treating or painting of the wood on (Government) "Red" Bridge.

Kamloops proper is semi-arid, but rainfall is very localized. While Kamloops proper would not have enough rainfall to grow its own Douglas fir, the area surrounding Kamloops does. The timber for the bridge was most likely harvested within 20 kilometres of the bridge site and transported either by land or by river. Red Bridge is very close to the confluence of the North and South Thompson Rivers. If any portion of the transport of the wood was by water, then the wood was immersed in water for a period, which would influence the longevity of the red hue.

The Ministry of Natural Resources employee had identified sunshine as a possible factor in wood weathering, so I investigated weather. A quick search reveals that Kamloops receives 316 days of sunshine each year, more than any city in central British Columbia (Current Results, n.d.).

Sunshine has both a drying and a bleaching effect over time. This increases greying speed. While it is difficult to be precise, suffice to say—Red Bridge would not have stayed red for long. It is possible the more protected underside of the bridge may have been red a bit longer. If we overestimate how long the wood used for the bridge may have had a red hue, we might generously say it was a red bridge for a year on the outer sides. Roughly 1,500 people (according to census data this was the approximate size of the population in 1887) might have referred to this as the Red Bridge. As mentioned earlier, in 1970 the railing by the walking lane on the bridge was painted bright red at the request of the Downtown Business Association. So, Red Bridge was provided a red railing, which justified the naming. The question remains, however: Is this story of wood colour the likely story for the name Red Bridge?

The Missing History

History is interesting, both for what is documented and for what is left out. There is additional history that is not shared in these historical documents. The "2 Rivers, 2 Peoples, 200 Years" slogan on the kiosk which serves as a summary of the region feels just a bit simplistic, although it certainly is optimistic. It does put the best face on this bridge and histories of bridge naming in Kamloops. Just as the history of residential schools, smallpox, and other impacts of colonization and exploitation emerge when we scratch below the surface into our deeply troubled histories with Indigenous peoples, the story of this bridge, and why there may be a red bridge and a white bridge, suggests the possibility of a darker side to this bridge naming. Red Bridge did connect the First Nations reserve (established in 1862) and the town. Land was confiscated from the Tk'emlúps Reserve to establish the bridge, as per the right to do this enshrined in the British North America Act. In the late 1800s it was not unusual for First Nations individuals to be known as "Red Indians." The *Sessional Papers* copied in Appendix 2 provide ample evidence of fear, racism, and a disregard for Indigenous people prior to the building of the bridge.

Is there a chance that the name "Red" Bridge had little to do with wood colouring and much to do with skin colour? Is there a chance that White Bridge was called this because this was the preferred bridge for white settlers in 1901? According to population data, Kamloops City had a population of 1,594 citizens in 1901 (First Nations people would not have been counted in this data) (Prentice, 2023). Data for another BC town, Lillooet, indicates the presence of "Indian Reserves" but does not include their population (Malaspina University-College, 2002). Why was there a need for two bridges, three kilometres apart, for a community with a population of 1,594 citizens? None of my research mentioned that white people were not allowed to use Red Bridge; in fact, it is quite clear this bridge was built to facilitate settlement and trade. Settlers could cross the bridge without issue, yet a second bridge, White Bridge, was built 14 years later. The next part of this search involved reading newspaper clippings that are available at the Kamloops Museum and searching the British Columbia *Sessional Papers* for clues.

British Columbia *Sessional Papers*

There is a treasure trove of information in the British Columbia *Sessional Papers*, currently stored electronically in the University of British Columbia Library's Open Collections. The records in this collection begin in about 1865. I reviewed the Public Accounts, from 1 July 1887 to 30 June 1888. The sessional paper states that D. F. Adams was awarded the construction of the Thompson River Bridge in Kamloops, for a total cost of $7,355.01, which included the making and painting of two sign boards for the bridge (cost of $15.00), and surveying, construction, materials, labour, advertising for tenders, etc. There is other sessional paper information that will be included later in the chapter.

There is a sessional paper called "Indian Land Question. 1850 – 1875." Some relevant letters are shared in Appendix 2. The descriptions of struggles with Indians, the ongoing nature of this across British Columbia but also directly in Kamloops, is clear. I mention a few highlights here but direct you to Appendix 2, where you may read for yourself some of the governmental history of relationships with Indigenous peoples in the province, and specifically, in the interior. In short, between 1850 and 1875 there is evidence of:

- Fear of hostile attitudes on the part of Indians toward white settlers in Cache Creek (26th December 1873)
- Concerns about grazing lands, leases, and the determination of Indian land (26th December 1873)
- Rumours of trouble with Indians east of the Cascades related to inadequate grazing land (27th December 1873)
- Threatened Indian attacks upon white settlers (12th January 1874)
- Council of Chiefs apparently voted seven to two in favour of war (Telegram, Clinton, January 9, 1874)

The papers indicate that all was not well, either for Indigenous peoples or for white settlers. There was considerable hostility that would have taken time to ignite and time to resolve.

Other Relevant Considerations

The Pass System of 1885

In 1885, in some parts of Canada, First Nations people needed passes from the Indian Agent to leave the reserve. The pass system was not part of the Indian Act but paralleled the act and was used to restrain First Nations. This extra-legal system, proposed by Hayter Reid to Edgar Dewdney and passed through various political hands and approved of by Prime Minister Macdonald, was instituted following the Métis Northwest Resistance (Rebellion). It served to segregate white settlers from Indigenous peoples and effectively imprisoned the Indigenous peoples on their reserves (Williams, 2015). It controlled who, among First Nations people, had permission to leave the reserve and limited the time spent off reserve, sometimes to as restrictive a time as "sunset." Should an individual be late returning to the reserve they could be fined or jailed. Its purpose was to prevent another rebellion from occurring but served as well to keep Indigenous people out of the towns and cities, and together with the residential school policies, was intended to force segregation. The pass system was never approved in the House of Commons, so was not legal. Although Sir John A. Macdonald knew this was not a legal policy, he put the system in place, and encouraged it to be kept secret, stating, as reported by Assistant Indian Commissioner Hayter Reed in 1893, that "all we can endeavor to do is to keep the true position from the Indians as long as possible" (Williams, 2015, 17:56). It was enacted.

The pass system matters. In Alex Williams' 2015 documentary film *The Pass System*, we learn that the implementation of the pass system marks "when you pass from one approach to First Nations people to another, to another, one in which the Canadian government feels safe, secure, settled and in charge and able to force its way forward" (13:57). It was primarily used in the prairie provinces of Alberta, Saskatchewan, and parts of Manitoba. The pass system ostensibly ended in 1941. All Indian agents were required to collect and send existing passes, old or current, to Dr. Harold McGill to be destroyed (37:33). Efforts to remove traces of the pass system were taken by requiring the collection of all existing passes. It was an extra-legal system, and evidence of it needed to be destroyed. However, the pass system did not end. Passes have been found that were issued as late as 1969. It should be noted that between the beginning of the pass system in 1885 and the beginning of the end of the pass system in 1941, the pass system informally approved by John A. Macdonald was not removed by the next ten prime ministers: Alexander Mackenzie, John Abbott, John Thompson, Mackenzie Bowell, Charles Tupper, Wilfrid Laurier, Robert Borden, Arthur

Meighen, William Lyon Mackenzie King, and R. B. Bennett (several had repeated terms as prime minister). It is safe to say the politicians all knew. None had trouble with this system. Was this long ago, as some claim, and was this extralegal system the only barrier faced by First Nations people? Did it have any influence on Kamloops, Secwepemcúlecw, building and/or naming Red Bridge, or any other local issue? Email correspondence does indicate "I have seen earlier Department of Indian Affairs agent reports about giving passes to non-indigenous men on the reserve, for example, after Tessie Celesta married John Dillabough, the Department of Indian Affairs agent would give him a written pass to walk on the reserve" (D. Jules, K. Favrholdt, G. Gottfriedson, personal communication, June 13, 2022). Overzealous Indian agents, like people who hold unchecked power any-where, did create issues. While some problems began with various civil and political servants, including a very ambitious elected official, Sir John A. Macdonald, these problems have lasted for now 150 years, not counting pre-Confederation issues, of which there were many.

Red Bridge was a vital connection between two communities: settlers and First Nations. Completed in 1887, two years after the implementation of the pass system in some parts of Canada, it eased travel and trade for settlers. One wonders: Beyond easing travel to farm and ranch land, as well as to Tk'emlúps Reserve, was it built to facilitate some travel to and from the Kamloops Industrial School, which opened in 1890, latterly referred to as the Kamloops Indian Residential School (Indian Residential School History and Dialogue Centre, n.d.)? If it was for trade, was the bridge built to facilitate what may have been a one-way trading relationship, settlers to Indigenous? Historically, if Indians wanted to sell something, they typi-cally needed permission from the Indian agent or farm instructor. Failing to get permission was worthy of a fine or even jail. The agent received all proceeds from selling things, when permitted. It was not permitted for there to be direct trade (Williams, 2015, 26:00). One example of the restric-tions applied to First Nations can be seen in this photo of a sign distributed in 1934. I encountered this sign at the Village of Clinton Museum, about an hour from Kamloops.

The pass system also meant parents from neighbouring First Nations could not travel to residential schools and retrieve their children—a pass would not be granted for this. The pass system was very useful to school authorities, as it greatly increased power over Indigenous peoples.

Beyond the commercial and other restrictions that Indian agents and other government officials imposed (and impose) on various activities, there are a few stories from Kamloops that fill in some information about the

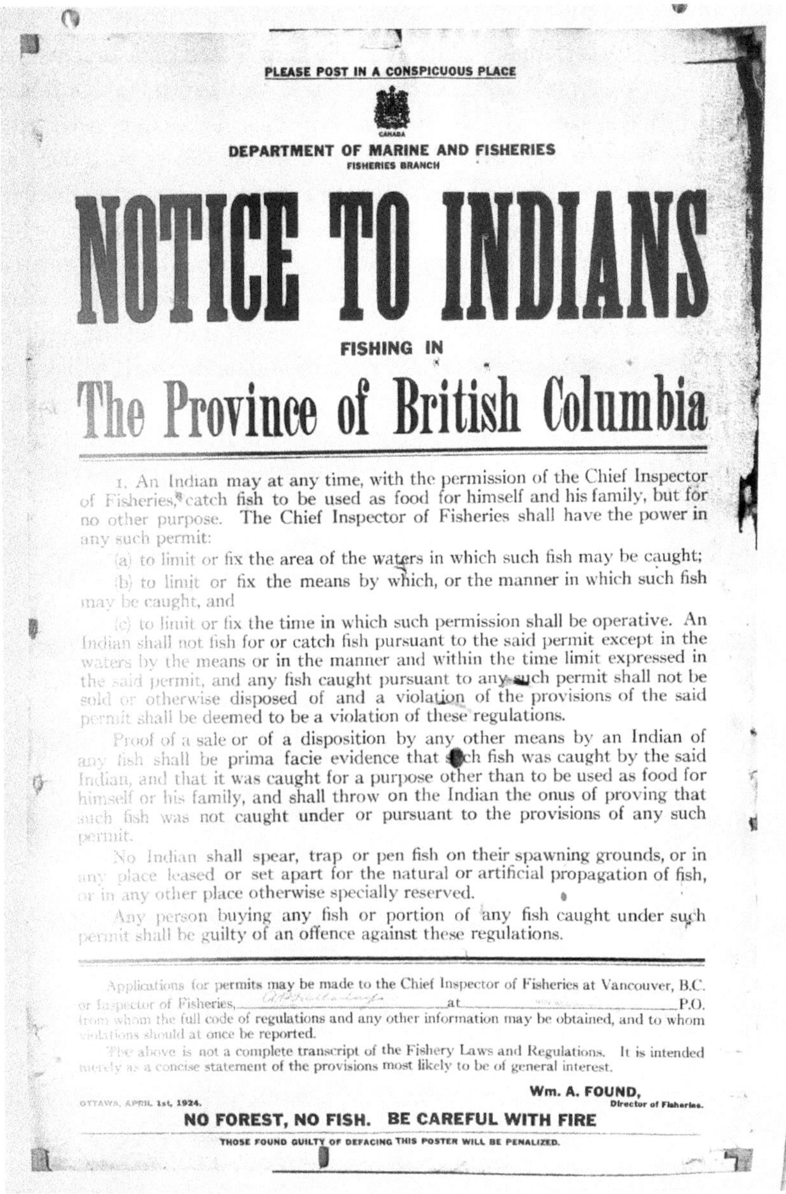

PLEASE POST IN A CONSPICUOUS PLACE

CANADA

DEPARTMENT OF MARINE AND FISHERIES
FISHERIES BRANCH

NOTICE TO INDIANS

FISHING IN

The Province of British Columbia

1. An Indian may at any time, with the permission of the Chief Inspector of Fisheries, catch fish to be used as food for himself and his family, but for no other purpose. The Chief Inspector of Fisheries shall have the power in any such permit:

(a) to limit or fix the area of the waters in which such fish may be caught;

(b) to limit or fix the means by which, or the manner in which such fish may be caught, and

(c) to limit or fix the time in which such permission shall be operative. An Indian shall not fish for or catch fish pursuant to the said permit except in the waters by the means or in the manner and within the time limit expressed in the said permit, and any fish caught pursuant to any such permit shall not be sold or otherwise disposed of and a violation of the provisions of the said permit shall be deemed to be a violation of these regulations.

Proof of a sale or of a disposition by any other means by an Indian of any fish shall be prima facie evidence that such fish was caught by the said Indian, and that it was caught for a purpose other than to be used as food for himself or his family, and shall throw on the Indian the onus of proving that such fish was not caught under or pursuant to the provisions of any such permit.

No Indian shall spear, trap or pen fish on their spawning grounds, or in any place leased or set apart for the natural or artificial propagation of fish, or in any other place otherwise specially reserved.

Any person buying any fish or portion of any fish caught under such permit shall be guilty of an offence against these regulations.

Applications for permits may be made to the Chief Inspector of Fisheries at Vancouver, B.C. or Inspector of Fisheries,_____at_____P.O. from whom the full code of regulations and any other information may be obtained, and to whom violations should at once be reported.

The above is not a complete transcript of the Fishery Laws and Regulations. It is intended merely as a concise statement of the provisions most likely to be of general interest.

Wm. A. FOUND,
Director of Fisheries.

OTTAWA, APRIL 1st, 1924.

NO FOREST, NO FISH.   BE CAREFUL WITH FIRE

THOSE FOUND GUILTY OF DEFACING THIS POSTER WILL BE PENALIZED.

FIGURE 5.3. Example of powers formally accorded to Indian agents.
Source: Victoria Handford.

bridge and the understandings of this bridge from the perspectives within the Nation of Tk'emlúps te Secwépemc. Garry Gottfriedson engaged in some discussions with Elder Gloria Sam, Elder Bertha Thomas, and Elder Teddy Gottfriedson (January 2023), each of whom shared some oral history of the bridge. To begin, the First Nations name for Red Bridge was Seme7 Bridge, which translates to "the white man's bridge." There were two hitching rails for Bennett wagons underneath Red Bridge. These were there as Indians were allowed to ride horses into town but could not bring Bennett wagons into town. If they drove a horse and wagon, it was hitched below the bridge—and left there until they returned for it. This would have hampered the potential for trade. Additionally, there were no sidewalks, which meant pedestrians were vulnerable to the horse and wagon traffic of the settlers, as the bridge was quite narrow. They did petition for a sidewalk, which was eventually created on one side of the bridge. And the bridge was sometimes the site of crimes. Garry's own grandfather was murdered on the bridge. His body was cast into the river. There was no investigation of this crime.

Other correspondence about Kamloops is also quite revealing:

> Kamloops had an area called "Chinatown" where the Indian Affairs Office was once located. In one of Mary Balf's books it shows that the townspeople went into an uproar when it was announced they were moving this office downtown. They said they did not want to see "the dirty Indians." Indian agents kept census records and detailed journals recording where Indians resided, who they married, the births of children and whether the child was legitimate or illegitimate, when, and how people died, if they went to jail and why, if they went to the Indian Residential School, and so on. Before WWII, laws prevented Indians from going into bars or consuming alcohol on the reserve and they were either fined or put in jail if they were caught. If a band chief or council member was caught consuming alcohol, the Indian Agent could remove him from office. (D. Jules, K. Favrholdt, G. Gottfriedson, personal communication, June 13, 2022)

Finally, in terms of historic perspectives found in the sessional paper titled "Papers Connected with the Indian Land Question 1850–1875," stored in the *Sessional Papers* at UBC, is the issue of concern about the size of reserve land allotted to Nations within Secwepemcúlecw, and concerns about warfare. I have copied the details into Appendix 2. It sheds light on issues within Secwepemcúlecw in 1874. While not direct, it does point toward issues that are historical, and that may provide understandings of past wrongs, and attitudes that existed.

Port Alberni Bridge, 2022

On September 27, 2022, CHEK News ran this headline: "Residential school survivors reclaim Alberni bridge they were banned from by painting it orange." The story was one of a residential school survivor and her husband, who spearheaded a campaign to paint the silver Port Alberni bridge orange. The bridge was a link between Port Alberni and the Tseshaht First Nation. The article states that the bridge has served as a reminder for the residential school survivors of the times when they were "trapped in Alberni Indian Residential school and the bridge they weren't allowed to cross to leave" (Ryan, 2022). On 1 October 2022, CHEK News printed a second story about the bridge titled "Port Alberni bridge honouring residential school survivors vandalized" (Brougham, 2022).

This vandalism was explicitly racist. These experiences of racism are not things of the past. They are daily occurrences in British Columbia and in Canada.

Conclusion

Given the pass system and other barriers, such as possible confinement to the reserve, the role of the residential school, the tremendous reach of Indian agents, the *Sessional Papers* indicating serious unrest in Kamloops and the surrounding communities, the naming by the Secwépemc people of Red Bridge as White Bridge, the eventual building of another "White Bridge" to service the settlers' needs, and the concerns of white and other settlers over the moving of the Department of Indian Affairs office, the very quick fading of Douglas fir given the location in the South Thompson River, the lack of treatment of the wood, the amount of sunshine, and how quickly this bridge would have turned grey, I am left asking two questions:

1. Is it likely that Red Bridge is referring to the colour of wood as the rationale for its name? Or,
2. Is there an alternative history, one where, as Bunch said when speaking about the history of Black people in America, "so much of our history is hidden in plain sight" (PBS NewsHour, 2016, 9:48)? Is it likely the bridge's name refers to a term freely used in days gone by, "Red Indian," because the bridge connected the town to the Indian reserve?

By following the historical threads of a given subject, Penelope Corfield identifies that people are living histories, and that history is inescapable. She claims that it is by studying our histories that we find connections through time, encouraging us to take a long view of connections. She states, "people will have access to a great human resource, compiled over many generations, which is the collective set of studies of the past, and the human story within that" (Corfield, 2007).

All the railing paint in the world, all the references to red hues in the wood, all the friendly expressions of "2 Rivers, 2 Peoples, 200 Years," do not convince me that the story of Red Bridge is complete. Whitewashing our history serves no one. To reconcile we must first name truth—and that truth will not necessarily be revealed in history books, because that truth is the preferred version as named by the dominant culture.

The name of the bridge needs to be changed. It is perpetuating a history of racism that is not disguised by historical plaques, red paint, or slogans. It is a barrier to reconciliation. Tell the truth. This is the first step in the Calls to Action. Then—plan for a shared, optimistic future.

References

British Columbia. Legislative Assembly. (1889). British Columbia. *Public Accounts for the Fiscal Year Ended 30th June, 1888. Period from 1st July, 1887, to 30th June, 1888.* https://dx.doi.org/10.14288/1.0062600

British Columbia. Legislative Assembly. (1887). *Report of the Chief Commissioner of Lamds [Lands] and Works of the Province of British Columbia, for the Year Ending 31st December 1886.* https://dx.doi.org/10.14288/1.0065785

Brougham, L. (2022, October 1). Port Alberni bridge honouring residential school survivors vandalized. *CHEK News.* https://www.cheknews.ca/bridge-honouring-residential-school-survivors-vandalized-1099065/

Corfield, P. J. (2007). *All people are living histories – which is why history matters.* Making History. https://archives.history.ac.uk/makinghistory/resources/articles/why_history_matters.html

Current Results. (n.d.). *Average Sunshine a Year in British Columbia.* https://www.currentresults.com/Weather/Canada/British-Columbia/sunshine-annual-average.php

Moloney, M. (2005, September 1). *"Those who suffer write the songs"—Remembering Frank Harte (1933-2005).* The Journal of Music. https://journalofmusic.com/focus/those-who-suffer-write-songs-remembering-frank-harte-1933-2005

Indian Residential School History and Dialogue Centre. (n.d.). *Kamloops (BC).* https://collections.irshdc.ubc.ca/index.php/Detail/entities/46

Malaspina University-College. (2002, March). *Population of British Columbia, 1901, according to electoral divisions.* https://hcmc.uvic.ca/~taprhist/content/documents/abstract1901.php

Ministry of Transportation and Highways. (1986). *Frontier to Freeway: A short, illustrated history of the roads in British Columbia.* British Columbia.

Mowat, F. (1979). *And No Birds Sang.* McClelland & Stewart.

PBS NewsHour (2016, September 21). *Full interview: Lonnie Bunch, director of Smithsonian African American History Museum.* https://www.pbs.org/newshour/nation/lonnie-bunch-present-future

Prentice, S. (2023, November 23). *Kamloops & Region Census Statistics: 1870–1971.* TRU Libraries. https://libguides.tru.ca/KamloopsRegionalCensus

Ryan, S. (2022). Residential school survivors reclaim Alberni bridge they were banned from by painting it orange. *CHEK News.* https://www.cheknews.ca/residential-school-survivors-reclaim-alberni-bridge-they-were-banned-from-painting-it-orange-1097278/

Stainton, C. (n.d.). *The North Shore Bridges of Kamloops.* https://exploreourshore.ca/the-bridges-of-kamloops/

The Kamloops Heritage Commission. (n.d.). *Red Bridge.* https://maps.kamloops.ca/Heritage/Photos/654%20LORNE%20ST.html

Western Canadian Heritage. *Red Bridge—Kamloops, BC.* https://www.waymarking.com/waymarks/wm14R09_Red_Bridge_Kamloops_BC

Williams, A. (2015). *The pass system: Life under segregation. In Canada.* http://thepasssystem.ca/home-2/

NEWCOMERS TO CANADA CALL TO ACTION

The Truth and Reconciliation Commission (2015, pp. 10–11) made two Calls to Action related to newcomers to Canada. Issues named as priorities for change in relation to Newcomers to Canada by the Calls to Action are:

93. We call upon the federal government, in collaboration with the national Aboriginal organizations, to revise the information kit for newcomers to Canada and its citizenship test to reflect a more inclusive history of the diverse Aboriginal peoples of Canada, including call upon the officials and host countries of information about the Treaties and the history of residential schools.
94. We call upon the Government of Canada to replace the Oath of Citizenship with the following:

> I swear (or affirm) that I will be faithful and bear true allegiance to Her Majesty Queen Elizabeth 11, Queen of Canada, Her Heirs and Successors, and that I will faithfully observe the laws of Canada including Treaties with Indigenous Peoples, and fulfill my duties as a Canadian citizen.

References

Truth and Reconciliation Commission of Canada. (2015). *Truth and Reconciliation Commission of Canada: Calls to Action.* https://ehprnh2mw03.exactdn.com/wp-content/uploads/2021/01/Calls_to_Action_English2.pdf

The Flesh of Ice

Garry Gottfriedson

river's frozen face
gnarled and jammed
thick ice skin
clear and sharp
reflections
stagnant in winter
crisp
crunching
snow
echoing footsteps
215 times
tromping
deceptive intentions
from the dorms to the river
picks and crow bars
weighing shoulders down
numb hands
sculpting
icy surfaces
lifeless bodies
roll out of woollen blankets
plunder frigid water
and jam beneath the flesh of ice
faces with forgotten names
sinking, sinking

Encounters

Fred Schaub

It's a thing with stories. They tend to sneak up on us, and we can't be sure when one ends and a new one begins until we look back to ponder the passage of time. I will start my story close to its end and then take us back to its beginning.

It was one of those early spring days. I knew spring was young, as its days did not quite know whether to be mild and sunny or cold and wet. As usual on my weekends I was out, floating in my weathered orange kayak. An insignificant orange speck within a wide ocean waterway in its endless hues of greens and blues. This was my way of soul care after a week of demanding work as a school administrator in the central coast of British Columbia. I mused, drifting serenely across the water.

Kayaking is a magical feeling of gliding across a watery cloud. This close to the water, our eyes make way for our ears, and we learn to listen to the environment around us long before our eyes are able to follow suit.

This particular morning the ocean was calm and inviting. Little did I know what was about to change for me.

However, to tell this whole story we have to go back 10 years, to its beginning:

It was one of those early fall days. I knew fall was young, as its days did not quite know whether to be mild and sunny or cold and wet. This was the day when I got closer to meeting a highly acknowledged Indigenous Elder in the interior of British Columbia. An Elder who was bestowed with many honours, including a doctorate by one of BC's renowned post-secondary institutions. At the time, I was in the middle of obtaining my education

FIGURE 6.1. From the heart; *left to right*: Fred Schaub, Garry Gottfriedson, and Patricia Liu Baergen.
Source: Victoria Handford.

degree. As a part of my studies, I chose to write a most significant historical account of World War II and its impact on the Indigenous peoples in the region where I lived.

Oh, how little I knew then.

As an immigrant to Canada, I was oblivious to any cultural protocols and expectations other than the colonizers' ways. So, I was quite surprised by the many obstacles I had to endure to provide this Elder this important opportunity of having her voice added to my most significant paper.

Oh, how little I knew then.

Finally, this early fall day, I was able to meet with the Elder's son in a local coffee shop. A yuppy place, with patrons all self-absorbed in their attempts to appear casual, soaking in those last summer-like rays. As I entered the café, it was not difficult to spot him, especially when hearing him call from across the room: "Hey! You must be the guy wanting to write about us. Here, have a seat!"

With this invitation, I met John. "Aren't you a bit old to be at university still?"

John continued with his keen sense of observation.

I seated myself across this man who showed the expected visual features of an Indigenous person of this region. Not that all Indigenous people are or look the same. However, after reading many books to study the region and its peoples' history, I felt confident in making this observation.

Oh, how little I knew then.

In a strange way, I started to feel at home within our conversation. It was filled with teasing and joking. It reminded me of something foreign but familiar. John told me many stories and historical facts but in a most unusual way. Not at all in the ways these facts and stories were presented in the academic articles and books of my studies.

In the middle of our conversation, John announced: "Mom must be about done with her council meeting, and we need to shuffle butt to meet her. I assume you are paying. Hah!"

Not expecting this, I was not ready for this meeting today; but in strange way, I felt fine in my unpreparedness.

John led the way in his family van, and I followed in my car. As we pulled off the main highway onto a gravelly road to the reserve, we passed the school-bus stop. Just then, the students got off the bus to walk the rest of the way to their homes on the reserve. John stopped and invited a couple of the kids to ride in his car, while announcing: "The rest of you hop in with the guy behind me, he won't mind!"

And with this, my car doors flew open. In no time my rusty Mercedes buckled under the load of countless children laughing, teasing, eating, and chattering; children I did not know.

As we arrived in front of the band office, John gave me that mischievous smile over his shoulder, while guiding three children out of his van. At that same time, there seemed to be a never-ending stream of children pouring out of my tired old car, each one giving me a wide smile and a friendly "Thanks man."

For the first time in my life, I was on a reserve. And, despite the many stories I had heard before, I felt welcome and safe. John guided me along to a group of adults, where I spotted his mom, the Elder I had been hoping to meet for weeks.

Now, I would love to tell you how I presented this Elder with a gift to show the expected respect, but I can't. I gave this Elder the respect, or the lack of it, as I knew to give to an older person from within the cultural norms I was raised.

Oh, how little I knew then.

What is left with me from this meeting is that soft touch of her warm-hearted and unconditional friendliness. With her calm but strong and precise voice, she thanked me for coming by and for my efforts to include her people in my paper. Turning to her son, she instructed him to lend me the manuscript of her not-yet published book to read. The Elder assured me that it contained some stories about World War II, and its impacts on her people. And to my greatest astonishment, she asked:

"Please make sure to bring it back in a few days, as we have to get it to the printer next week, and this is the only copy I have."

The best I could scratch together was a measly "Thank you."

Oh, how little I knew then.

So, this was the beginning of my story. To end it we now move forward those 10 years, with me sitting in my orange kayak.

Over those past years, I was privileged with the gift of many experiences and learnings. I was adopted into two Haiłzaqv families and felt at home within this remote coastal territory of the Haiłzaqv Nation.

My kayak carved into the dark sheet of watery glass in front of me yet leaving no trace behind, paddle stroke by paddle stroke.

In this serenity, my ears picked up that familiar and rhythmic sound of an ocean mammal's breathing: "Pf-tsch...(pause)...pf-tsch..."

My ears told me that this was the breathing of a porpoise that was still outside the range of my eyes. It was coming closer. As my eyes caught up to my ears, I was able to spot the porpoise, with its continuous rhythm of: "Pf-tsch...(pause)...pf-tsch..."

While I observed the porpoise's rhythmic surfacing, I realized it was adjusting its course and curving toward me. It was obviously ignoring the Department of Fisheries and Oceans' rule of staying 100 metres away from any vessel.

Once the porpoise drew closer, it surfaced 10 feet to my right, then dove again under the tip of my kayak. Before coming back up, it broke its chain of rhythm and bumped my kayak's tip with its flipper. Emerging from its shallow dive, its eyes locked with mine, and we recognized each other, alone in this watery element, as two living beings coming together. In this moment I felt the land, this territory recognizing me, and I began to understand my place in it.

What is left with me is the soft touch of a living being that altered its path to gift me with its presence.

It is impossible for me to think of this experience without thinking of my meeting with the Elder 10 years earlier.

What I was not yet able to grasp then meeting the Elder, was laid out clearly for me in the encounter with this porpoise:

Regardless of who we are. Regardless of where we come from. Regardless of where we hope to go. To live together we need to come together unconditionally. We need to use our eyes to look into our hearts, allowing us to be together in a genuine way. And we need to do so without our lenses, without our preconceptions, just us.

Oh, how little I knew then. Much remains to learn.

Reconciliation and Decolonization: From the Shadows of Settler Shame to the Generosity of an Ethical Relationality

Fred Schaub

> Understanding is the existential being of the own most potentiality of being of Dasein itself in such a way that this being discloses in itself what its very being is about.
> Heidegger, 1953/2010, p. 140

Abstract

Based on the concept of "ethical space," as defined by Willie Ermine (2007, 2011), this chapter examines the complexities of finding ourselves and each other as common relations within Dwayne Donald's (2009, 2013, 2016, 2021) space of "ethical relationality." I attend to our struggles as non-Indigenous participants in such relationships to ascertain our identities and to reconcile our inherent roles within divergent perceptions. I then highlight the historic and current continuum of colonization as an impediment to entering such an ethical relationality, by emphasizing the influence of self-identifiers such as "settlers," with their correlation to guilt or shame. Different modifications of such deprecating self-identifiers will be examined as potential barriers to such an ethical relationality. Within this spirit of bringing together and walking in two worlds, I attempt to ground my writing within the wisdom of Indigenous and non-Indigenous teachers and knowledge keepers.

Call to Action 63 iii and iv, in the *Final Report* of the Truth and Reconciliation Commission of Canada (Truth and Reconciliation Commission of Canada [TRC], 2015), calls on the "Council of Ministers of Education, Canada to maintain an annual commitment to Aboriginal education issues" (p. 238). While this call is directed to the Council of Ministers of Education in Canada, we as leaders, teachers, and scholars in education carry a responsibility to support this call—in our leadership, instruction, research, and publications. Our abilities and readiness to relate to this historic and current continuum of colonization are at distinct stages—they reflect our personal journeys and cannot be legislated through laws or policies. In the speaker series "Namesakes, Responsibilities, and Academia," Dwayne Donald quotes Dr. Leroy Little Bear to describe an identification crisis of some individuals who walk on the land: "You know you have an identification problem, when the land does not recognize you" (2021).

As non-Indigenous and Indigenous humans, our recognition of the land and the land of us is an essential step on our journeys toward the decolonization of who we are and what we do. Every non-Indigenous person on this land has come from somewhere else. While some have the deeper roots of their families living for generations in Canada, and others have arrived a few years or days ago, we all must reconcile our presence within this land before being able to reconcile with our responsibilities. For this land to recognize us, we first must resolve who we are for this land.

In this chapter, I examine the impact of "settler shame" on our ability to recognize the land we walk on and to be recognized by this land. I apply the findings of perception patterns, as different interpretations of the same occurrences, and the divergence of these patterns along cultural lines. This will illuminate the significance and the possibilities of "ethical space" (Ermine, 2007, 2011; Pritchard, 2020) or "ethical relationality" (Donald, 2009, 2013, 2016, 2021).

"Welcome, My Name is Fred. I am a Settler..."

Cuthand (2021) claims that by introducing ourselves as settlers, we, as non-Indigenous individuals, create a division, a hierarchy, at the outset of any interaction: "If we are trying to be on equal ground, why are you pointing out the hierarchy of colonizer and colonized as soon as we meet? Even what defines a settler includes the act of colonizing. Canada is a product of settler colonialism" (p. 1). This struggle of self-identification for non-Indigenous individuals here in Canada seems ongoing, especially after the hearings and events of the Truth and Reconciliation Commission in Canada and its findings between 2009 and 2015. Call to Action 63 iii and iv (TRC, 2015) asks for: "Building student capacity for intercultural understanding, empathy, and mutual respect," with a focus on the training of educators. In view of this identification struggle, it will be difficult, if not impossible, to fulfill such a Call to Action before we, as non-Indigenous individuals, resolve our struggles of knowing who we are within this relationship, and learn how to introduce ourselves to others and the land without creating or broadening an unintended hierarchical divide.

I have struggled with my identification as an immigrant to this country, especially as it relates to this land and the Indigenous peoples who have lived on this land since time immemorial. Who am I to this land and who am I to the peoples of this land?

Rozin (2003) states that "cultural differences between cultures A and B, as represented in narratives, rituals, customs, and descriptions by ethnographers, are generally bigger than the actual differences between individuals in the two cultures" (p. 274). I can attest to this through my experience of living and working within the unceded territories of the Haiłzaqv Nation, where I had the honour of being adopted into two families. When contemplating my identity within this relationship, my late mentor, Elder and aunt Phyllis McKay (personal communication, 2010 to 2016), guided me: "You are one of us, because it matters little what flows through your heart, it only matters what is in your heart; and what is in your heart makes you one of us."

This experience alone makes it impossible for me to self-identify as a settler to this land. First, it would dishonour the memory and teachings of my aunt Phyllis, and it would debase the honour bestowed on me and my family by my brothers and sister who asked us to be a part of their families. Second, it would trap me within the guilt or shame of a dark history. For us who are non-Indigenous, our individual relationships to this land and its peoples guide our positionality within the relationship between all. Do we veil ourselves within the shame and guilt of colonialism, or do we expose ourselves to the vulnerabilities of a journey toward an ethical space (Ermine, 2007, 2011; Pritchard, 2020); ethical relationality (Donald, 2009, 2013, 2016, 2021)?

The Association for Canadian Studies (Jedwab, 2019) looked at Canadians' pride in their country's history in view of the agreement that a genocide was committed on Indigenous peoples in Canada. One of the most significant findings was that if the Strongly agree and Somewhat agree columns are added together, 53.1 percent of Canadians strongly agreed that Indigenous people in Canada were the victims of genocide and 33.2 percent of individuals identified they were proud of Canada's history. As one does not assume that those Canadians are proud of acts of genocide, these numbers reveal a disassociation between those acts and their perceived history of Canada. The same survey revealed that most Canadians perceive this genocide to have been committed mainly by British and French founders and the churches, and largely absolve the Canadian government, of the time and of today, of these acts of genocide (see table 16.2).

TABLE 16.1. Settler Guilt or Settler Shame: A Free Pass?

		Indigenous peoples in Canada have been the victims of a genocide			
		Strongly agree	Somewhat agree	Somewhat disagree	Strongly disagree
	Strongly agree	17.8%	15.4%	23.7%	37.7%
I am proud of Canada's history	Somewhat agree	35.3%	57.7%	56.6%	45.9%
	Somewhat disagree	34.0%	20.8%	13.9%	8.9%
	Strongly disagree	10.1%	2.0%	2.2%	4.2%
	No Answer	2.8%	4.2%	3.6%	3.1%

Source: Jedwab, 2019.

Regan (2010) asks us to disrupt that naive view of Canadian history, which is based on a view of settlers being hardworking and upstanding. In addition, it often considers the colonialist brutality of the residential school system as a mere aberration within that history. This distorted view is reflected in table 16.1 and raises the question: Does our self-identification as settlers refer to this romantic take on a settler in their little house on the prairies? Or is that settler identification rooted within the darker aspects of genocide, of land appropriation, of settler guilt and shame?

In the attempt to answer this question, it is relevant to consider the terms "guilt" and "shame." Shame represents a painful feeling about oneself, often not related to a specific act, while guilt describes the feeling resulting from a more specific, wrongful act. Shame would then be the more appropriate term to describe the anguish of being associated with colonialism, including genocide. I will use the term "settler shame" for the remainder of this chapter. Kizuk (2020) claims that: "Settler shame desperately seeks resolution, preferring to re-establish the self as good, or worthy of pride, rather than respond to other-oriented concerns of justice. As such, settler shame maintains a settler colonial system of oppression" (p. 162).

When introducing ourselves as settlers, we take claim of the "us" within the interaction. We set a narrowly defined perimeter of our own being, and we do so with our heads bowed as the other on someone else's land. While placing us within this abstruseness of shame, it also provides us with some comforts of control. Ahmed (2005) writes: "As I have shown, the desire to feel good or better can involve the erasure of relations of violence [The] expression of shame about histories of violence work[s] not only as a narrative of 'recovery' but also as a form of 'covering over'" (p. 83). Table 16.1 shows how Ahmed's explanation of covering over becomes evident. Despite all the negative connotations of settling, colonizing, and genocide, there seems to be solace within the belonging to a majority, to a proud Canadian settler history.

> What is striking is how shame becomes not only a mode of recognition of injustices committed against others, but also a form of nation building. It is shame that allows us "to assert our identity as a nation." Recognition works to restore the nation or reconcile the nation to itself by "coming to terms with" its own past in the expression of "bad feeling." But in allowing us to feel bad, does shame also allow the nation to feel better? What is the relation between the desire to feel better and the declaration of bad feeling? (Ahmed, 2005, p. 72)

On June 11, 2008, the prime minister of Canada, the Right Honourable Stephen Harper, apologized for the historic wrongdoings in Canada that saw generations of Indigenous children ripped from their families and put into residential schools. Those children were exposed to atrocities under authorization and supervision, direct or indirect, by the Canadian government, in a strategically planned attempt to expunge the Indian in the child (Tait, 2022). This apology initiated the journey of the Canadian Truth and Reconciliation Commission across Canada between 2009 and 2015 to listen and to bear witness to stories of residential school survivors. This process initiated a broader awareness of the atrocities, resulting in a nationwide feeling of shame.

Here is where we must return to the difference between shame and guilt. Shame allows us to feel badly about something that happened in the past—something we did not control—something that we need to carry for perpetrators of this past. Table 16.2 highlights how non-Indigenous members of this nation have immersed themselves in the comforts of this shame. They have assigned the responsibility for their shame to the most irreproachable groups of our past—the founders, the settlers, and the churches. They do not assign shame to the government. They assign the guilt of their shame to groups to whom they can refer to as those "others."

TABLE 16.2. Assigned Blame for Injustices toward Indigenous Peoples

	Canadians Asked			
Responses Provided	*Total*	*French*	*English*	*Other*
All Canadians	21%	22%	22%	16%
The British and French that founded Canada	32%	26%	33%	40%
Catholic and Protestant Churches	25%	30%	24%	20%
The government / the Canadian Government / the government of the time	1%	1%	1%	2%
The Indigenous populations / themselves	1%	0%	1%	0%
Other	3%	2%	4%	3%
I prefer not to answer	16%	19%	14%	29%

Source: Jedwab, 2019.

While finding that solace within this communal shame about this historic guilt assigned so conveniently onto others, the question that needs to be asked now is: Who carries the guilt for the indignations of today, including the number of incarcerations and children in care, or the graduation rates in our public and independent schools? Maybe it is time to step out of the shadow and perception of past shame, and work through our share of current guilt.

Perceptions Across a Divide

> Your perception may not be my reality.
> Kala, 2011

In examining the statistics in tables 16.1 and 16.2, we see individuals' perceptions compiled into a perception pattern of an average population.

Perception is our individual ability to gain awareness of a phenomenon through our senses, through our lenses. Our perceptions are then rooted in our axiological, ontological, and epistemological development from our earliest childhood. While we have little influence on our upbringing and the values we have acquired, we can examine our self, our current values, and our perceptions of the world around us. We have the ability to modify and adjust those perceptions as we move forward. Probably the most exacting task on this path is the recognition that the reality we see is our perceived reality, not an unshakable truth.

TABLE 16.3. Research Participants

| | Group size | |
Research participant group	*Indigenous*	*Non-Indigenous*
Current/recent students (Grade 12)	2	0
Parents of current/recent students	2	0
Teachers and support workers	2	2
Community Members/Administrators	2	3
Senior Management, Trustee (school district)	0	3
Total	**16 research participants**	

Source: Fred Schaub.

As an example of such a perception pattern I would like to shift our focus to my research of an apparent education gap between Indigenous and non-Indigenous learners in a public Kindergarten to Grade 12 education setting (Schaub, 2020). Using narrative, semi-structured interviews with 16 participants (table 16.3), I was able to discern perception patterns between different participants along seven main educational topics (see Appendix 3): Community; Culture; Support; Statistics; Trust; Attendance; Isolation.

The narrative interviews revealed three to six themes or perceptions for each of the seven main topics. Using the example of the main topic of "culture," four such themes or perceptions were identified: cultural diversity celebrated, culture used within colonial system (education focused), cultural diversity identified, and cultural understanding needed.

Using the data, I established perception patterns (thematic patterns) under each one of the seven basic topics. Each pattern reflected an account of the themes as each research participant expressed them.

In a broad generalization, the patterns in this example show a significant semblance to the patterns revealed within the other six basic topics (see Appendix 3). Regarding the basic topic of culture, eight non-Indigenous participants expressed that Indigenous culture is celebrated in our schools 15 times, while only one Indigenous participant expressed this theme once. This Indigenous participant referred to an experience of celebrating cultural difference from their childhood in New Zealand. What I was able to discern was the significantly different perceptions between the Indigenous and non-Indigenous research participant groups as expressed through the four themes mentioned above.

While there is a need to celebrate, identify, invite, and understand Indigenous culture in our schools, there is an apparent dissonance along the lines of Indigenous and non-Indigenous participants and their perceptions regarding how well that need is addressed in our schools. A dissonance of such significance along cultural lines can last only in an environment where those two population groups remain apart, where there is little to no open and unguarded communication about those patterns across this apparent education gap. Elder Flora Sampson (2022) reminds us that "to reconcile, we need unity, we need to come together."

From Settler Shame and Perceptional Confinements toward an Ethical Relationality

Hilistis (2022), Elder Pauline Waterfall, tells us that "[t]here is no hierarchy in humanness, no matter if we are purple, blue, or green, we all are the same. We breathe, we eat, we cry, we love. We all are one." This same sentiment was expressed in the words of Elder Minnie Manuel (2022) when she urged her audience that we all are the same, and we need to come together as one. Donald (2009) writes:

> What are required are curricular and pedagogical engagements that traverse the divides of the past and present. Such work must contest this denial of historic, social, and curricular relationality by asserting that the perceived civilizational frontiers are actually permeable and that perspectives on history, memory, and experience are connected. (p. 5)

Donald considers his statement within the concept of an ethical space, as defined by Ermine (2007), and terms this space an ethical relationality. Ermine (2007) refers to the encounter of Indigenous and Western ways as the encounter between "thought worlds" (p. 201). It appears then that we are caught within our "thought worlds" or "perceived civilizational frontiers" (p. 201). We are caught in our own perceptions of our systemic and institutionalized worlds. In a 2011 video interview, Ermine (2011) talks about ethical space as a common ground, where we move from those "thought worlds" and perceptions to seeing each other as humans. Ermine asserts that "when we take all these institutional or systemic webs and curtains out, we start to see our humanity."

The concept of settler shame, in its relation to our identity as a nation and a mode to feel better within our nation's history (Ahmed, 2005), can be interpreted as such institutional webs or curtains that need to be removed and opened to allow us to see each other as humans, as one of all.

German philosopher Hans-Georg Gadamer (1975/2015) professes, "belonging to traditions belongs just as originally and essentially to the historical finitude of Dasein as does its projectedness toward future possibilities of itself" (p. 262). As we draw back those curtains it is important for us to be certain and grounded in who we are and where we come from, as much as it is important for us to remain open to those future possibilities of our own being (*Dasein*).

As one first step in the process of reconciliation, it is then important to establish a space, an ethical space and ethical relationality, where such reconciliation can happen in togetherness instead of isolation. Gadamer (2015) contemplates this difficult task of understanding each other:

> To comprehend ourselves within the world. I did say that this is actually the topic. And this means: To comprehend ourselves with each other, and to comprehend each other with ourselves, this means to understand the other. And this is morally not logical; the most difficult task of all.

According to Gadamer, it is much easier to remain within our perceptions of the world and its society and to perceive the other as an other.

When drawing back those systemic and institutionalized curtains, woven on the loom of Western colonialization, we will encounter resistance. One of the strongest forces hindering this drawing back will be our own fears of vulnerability—the fear of exposing ourselves to that other, together with a possible fear of seeing that other within their vulnerabilities. "All new discovery takes place not on the basis of complete concealment but takes its point of departure from discoveredness in the mode of semblance" (Heidegger, 1953/2010, p. 213).

Linda Tuhiwai Smith (2012) explains the complexity of colonization: "It was not just Indigenous populations that had to be subjugated. Europeans also needed to be kept under control, in service of the greater imperial enterprise" (p. 24). This burden of indoctrination, carried by all, adds considerable weight to those curtains.

It becomes apparent that a Call to Action, such as 63 iii and iv (TRC, 2015), requires much more than an annual commitment by the Council of Ministers of Education, Canada, to Aboriginal education issues. To use Hilistis's (2022) words, "no matter if we are purple, blue, or green," we all need to come together, and the first step on this journey will be our own reconciliation with our personal curtains—curtains, such as settler shame and our perceptions of the other.

> I often think about how Jesus said that he gave us a new commandment that was greater than all the others: to love one another as he loved us. How the hell did those goddamn priests and others rationalize their actions? It is beyond embarrassing. It makes me sick for all those that were put through the pain that the church inflicted. It is a shame that runs so deep. It is my job to live with that shame as part of my identity. (Student statement in *Issues in Aboriginal Education* at Vancouver Island University, 2022)

The sentiments and inner turmoil expressed in the preceding quotation are of deep shame. This shame makes it impossible for us to attempt any steps toward reconciliation across the two worlds. We must first reconcile the shame within. An inner reconciliation lifts the burdens of shame from our shoulders, freeing us to take the next steps on our personal journeys toward the outside, toward the other.

Drawing back the curtains requires a much more complex process than simply pulling on a cord one day. To prepare ourselves for an ethical relationality, a space where we can come together and openly state our perceptions, while learning and accepting others, we need to ready ourselves. We need to be willing and able to accept other ways of viewing or perceiving the same phenomenon within Gadamer's (2015) way of unconditional understanding: "To comprehend ourselves with each other, and to comprehend each other with ourselves, this means to understand the other."

Within an ethical relationality, we need to be able to enlarge our axiological lenses—our values and value judgments. We need to expand our ontological lenses—our perceptions of existence and reality. Lastly, we need to spread our epistemological lenses—our base, nature, and reason of knowledge. Most of all, we need to learn to trust our own being in its ability to accept openly and grow through such acceptance. Only then can we safely and purposefully start drawing those curtains. Donald (2016) applies the wisdom of Cree Elders and their teaching. He explains the term *wicihitowin* as describing the "life-giving energy that is generated when people face each other as relatives and build trusting relationships by connecting with others in respectful ways" (p. 10).

Conclusion

Elder Mike Arnouse (2022) reminds us that "we can discuss forever and write as many books as we want; but at one point, we need to start the healing process." Concepts such as guilt and shame cannot stand without pain and hurt. The raw pain expressed in the earlier statement by a young undergraduate student shows the deep shame and anger that our history of colonialization, in its worst excesses, can arouse in many non-Indigenous stakeholders in this inherited past. While our inner journey from such raw emotions to a place of ethical relationality might appear as insuperable, it also can offer us a path to solace—a path to an inner understanding that will allow us to reach out to the other, to draw back those curtains.

In my experience as an educator, I have had the great fortune of spending time with many Indigenous Elders and knowledge keepers on my journey of learning. Through this process of self-discovery, I came to understand the need to reconcile feelings of shame and anger, which were explained to me as lazy emotions that keep us from dealing with the tasks at hand. While I know intellectually that this is not my shame or anger to carry, deep inside me those feelings tend to flare up, often when least expected. It is in these moments when I need to trust my path and the concept of an ethical relationality.

As we look at a Call to Action such as 63 iii and iv (TRC, 2015), we need to understand that such a call reaches far beyond policies and guidelines or an annual commitment by the intergovernmental Council of Ministers of Education, Canada. This call can only be fulfilled by us individuals as an ongoing commitment, in everything we do. Intercultural understanding, empathy, and mutual respect cannot be legislated or passed on through curriculum; they need to be experienced, modelled, and lived, both inside and beyond the classroom, and become a part of who we are as human beings on our journeys.

> Wanderer, the road is your
> footsteps, nothing else;
> wanderer there is no pain
> you lay down a path in
> walking.
> In walking you lay down a
> path
> and when turning around
> you see the road you'll
> never step on again.
> Wanderer, path there is none,
> only tracks on ocean foam.
> (Machado, in Varela, 1987, p. 63)

References

Ahmed, S. (2005). The politics of bad feeling. *Australian Critical Race and Whiteness Studies Association Journal*, 1, 72–85.

Arnouse, M. (2022, April 8). Secwépemc Elder, addressing a writers retreat at Quaaout Lodge, Chase, BC, Canada.

Cuthand, S. (2021, August 30). Introducing yourself as a "settler" creates division. *CBC News*. https://www.cbc.ca/news/canada/saskatoon/calling-yourself-a-settler-pov-1.6151582

Donald, D. (2009). Forts, curriculum, and Indigenous métissage: Imagining decolonization of aboriginal-Canadian relation in educational contexts. *First Nations Perspectives*, 2(1), 1–24.

Donald, D. (2013). On making love to death: Plains Cree and Blackfoot wisdom. In Smith, M. S. (Ed.), *Transforming the academy: Indigenous education, knowledges and relations* (pp.14–18). University of Edmonton.

Donald, D. (2016). From what does ethical relationality flow? An "Indian" act in three artifacts. *Counterpoints* 478, 10–16.

Donald, D. (2021, August 21). Episode 3: Namesakes, responsibilities, and academia [Video]. *Presenting our Presence*. YouTube. https://www.youtube.com/watch?v=tDgvC4avQDk

Ermine, W. (2007). The ethical space of engagement. *Indigenous Law Journal* 6(1), 193–203.

Ermine, W. (2011). Willie Ermine: What is ethical space? [Video]. *Different Knowings*. YouTube. https://www.youtube.com/watch?v=85PPdUE8Mbo

Gadamer, H.-G. (2015). Hans Georg Gadamer: entender y entenderse (understand and understanding) [Video]. *Un centauro en el desierto*. YouTube. https://www.youtube.com/watch?v=YUYfWKEs1wE

Gadamer, H.-G. (1975/2015). *Truth and method* (J. Weinsheimer & D. G. Marshall, Trans.). Bloomsbury Academic.

Heidegger, M. (1953/2010). *Being and Time* (translated by Joan Stambaugh). State University of New York Press.

Hilistis, Waterfall, P. (2022, April 4). Haiłzaqv Elder, addressing an undergraduate class at Victoria Island University, Nanaimo, BC, Canada.

Jedwab, J. (2019). Canadian opinion on whether a genocide was committed against Indigenous Peoples in Canada? Association for Canadian Studies. https://acs-aec.ca/wp-content/uploads/2019/06/ACS-Indigenous-Peoples-and-Genocide-in-Canada-EN.pdf

Kala, A. (2011). *Life.. Love.. Kumbh..* Srishti Publisher & Distributors.

Kizuk, S. (2020). Settler shame: A critique of the role of shame in settler-indigenous relationships in Canada. *Hypatia* 35, 161–177.

Manuel, M. (2022, April 8). Secwépemc Elder, addressing a writers retreat at Quaaout Lodge, Chase, BC, Canada.

Pritchard, G. (2020). *Indigenous place making and ethical space.* 4 Directions of Conservation Consulting Services. https://cela.ca/wp-content/uploads/2020/11/Indigenous-Place-Making-Ethical-Space.pdf

Regan, P. (2010). *Unsettling the settler within: Indian residential schools, truth telling, and reconciliation in Canada.* UBC Press.

Rozin, P. (2003). Five potential principles for understanding cultural differences in relation to individual differences. *Journal of Research in Personality* 37, 273–283.

Sampson, F. (2022, April 8). Secwépemc Elder, addressing a writers retreat at Quaaout Lodge, Chase, BC, Canada.

Schaub, A. (2020). *Examining an apparent educating gap between non-indigenous and indigenous learners: A hermeneutic phenomenology approach* [Doctoral thesis, University of Calgary]. http://hdl.handle.net/1880/112648

Smith, T. L. (2012). *Decolonizing methodologies* (2nd ed.) St. Martin's Press.

Tait, L. (2022, February 28). Addressing an undergraduate class at Vancouver Island University, Nanaimo, BC, Canada.

Truth and Reconciliation Commission of Canada [TRC]. (2015). *Honouring the truth, reconciling for the future: Summary of the final report of the Truth and Reconciliation Commission of Canada.* https://ehprnh2mwo3.exactdn.com/wp-content/uploads/2021/01/Executive_Summary_English_Web.pdf

Varela, F. (1987). Laying down a path in walking. In Thompson, W. I. (Ed.), *GAIA: A way of knowing— political implications of the new biology.* Lindisfarne Press.

Exploring Curriculum as a Lived Experience of Poetic Dwelling in between Place Stories

Patricia Liu Baergen

Abstract

In this chapter, I explore curriculum as a lived experience of poetic dwelling in between place stories. Through a form of poetic inquiry that juxtaposes poetry and autobiographical narratives of place, I aim to decolonize my immigrant and settler lived experience by considering the Truth and Reconciliation Commission's Calls to Action 63 iii and 93 (2015). Also, as a curriculum researcher, to understand contemporary Canadian curriculum studies in response to the 94 Calls to Action, I believe it is important to return to the questioning of the historical present that juxtaposes history, society, and subjectivity. To question the colonial historical present in Canada, I attune to the Indigenous curriculum scholar Dwayne Donald's call for the relationality of lived curriculum and place pedagogy. In response to Donald's call, I return to my autobiographical narratives of place stories to seek the meaning of my immigrant settler's being and belonging and to disrupt the binary thinking of identity politics that is embedded in the settler's colonialism of curriculum-as-plan. Through the juxtaposed story of places, I hope that languages and the freedom of poetic ruminations can engage in a never-ending conversation and a new layer of understanding of our lived curriculum of being-in-the-world or transcend the curriculum space of being-beyond-earthly-world.

FIGURE 6.2. Writing in action with Elder Flora Sampson and Patricia Liu Baergen. *Source*: Victoria Handford.

Curriculum is many things to many people. (Aoki, 1978/2005, p. 94)

Curriculum-as-plan is an abstraction yearning to come alive in the presence of teachers and students. What it lacks is situatedness. A situated curriculum is a curriculum-as-lived. It is curriculum in the presence of people and their meanings. It is an experienced curriculum. I like to call it the first-order curriculum world. (Aoki, 1986a/1991/2005, p. 231)

The word "curriculum," for many practising teachers, is understood as a set of documents that the school district office requires them to teach, and these documents are published in scope and sequence guides by the provincial ministry of education in Canada. For many prospective teachers, curriculum denotes a course syllabus. Alongside these literal and institutional meanings of curriculum-as-plan (Aoki, 1986b/2005), often embedded with the political agenda of the government, curriculum is a "highly symbolic concept" (Pinar & Reynolds, 1992, p. 847). However, many teachers know that there is another curriculum world—curriculum-as-lived (Aoki, 1986b/2005)—situated amid the lived experiences of teachers and students in classroom. In one important sense, the school curriculum is what older generations choose to tell younger generations (Pinar & Reynolds, 1992). Whatever the school subject, the curriculum is always situated in the juxtaposition of the historical, political, racial, gendered, phenomeno-logical, autobiographical, aesthetic, theological, and international context. Learning in between the tension of two curriculum worlds—curriculum-as-plan and curriculum-as-lived—curriculum becomes "the site on which the generations struggle to define themselves and the world" (Pinar et al., 1995, p. 847–848). As a Taiwanese-Canadian, a teacher, and a curriculum researcher living, teaching, learning, and researching the meaning of my being and my belonging to an Indigenous ancestral land, I become part of a complicated curriculum conversation involving history, society, and subjectivity (Pinar, 2012).

In this chapter, I explore curriculum as a lived experience of poetic dwelling in between place stories. Through a form of poetic inquiry that juxtaposes poetry and autobiographical narratives of place stories, I hope to decolonize my immigrant settler's lived experience by considering Calls to Action 63 iii and 93 made by the Truth and Reconciliation Commission of Canada (2015). Also, as a curriculum researcher, to understand contem-porary Canadian curriculum studies in response to the 94 Calls to Action, I believe it is important to return to the questioning of the historical pres-ent that juxtaposes history, society, and subjectivity.

The historical present of Canada is situated in the history of colonial-ism, Asian immigrants on the West Coast, and African American refugees on the Atlantic Coast. This "settlers' land" carries a "linguistic and politi-cal complexity" that lives on today (Liu Baergen, 2020). In such complexity, Dwayne Donald, an Indigenous curriculum scholar, pointed out that "the key challenge facing Indigenous peoples today is the assertion of differ-ence in response to the homogenizing power of coloniality, neoliberalism, and globalization" (2009, p. xvii). Although focusing on difference, Donald reminded us that this complexity seems in "contradiction to Indigenous philosophical emphasis on holism and ecological relationality" (p. xvii). In turn, the question Donald put forth for educators is: "How can we be simul-taneously different and related" (p. xvii)? In light of Donald's call for the relationality of lived curriculum and place pedagogy, I return to my auto-biographical narratives of place stories to seek the meaning of my being and belonging and to disrupt the binary thinking of identity politics that is embedded in the settler colonialism of curriculum-as-plan. Through the juxtaposed story of places, I hope that languages and the freedom of poetic ruminations can engage in a never-ending conversation and a new layer of understanding of our lived curriculum of being-in-the-world or transcend the curriculum space of being-beyond-earthly-world.

還至本處

泰雅的織布有如一篇史詩
訴說 著傳承的故事
聆聽 彩虹橋 七彩的天籟
川梭 泰雅的 織布機
介於 古老菱紋線 與 眼睛 之間
找尋 那條 回家的路
回歸 與祖靈 相遇 的初始

Coming Home and Home Coming

Atayal weaving is an epic
Whispering the stories of Rainbow Bridge
Listening to the heavenly sound of seven colours of Hongu Utux
Weaving through rhythm of ancient Atayal's Wubun
In between the ancient diagrams and ancestors' eyes
Finding the way home
To return to the ancestral place where we depart
To return to the ancestral place where we come

Epic One: Taiwan, Taipei, and Wulai

I guess, I was on a search for the inner meaning of my *isness*. (Aoki, 1979/2005, p. 336)

...moving away from the abstraction of theory and attuning to the significance of personhood is educational. (Liu Baergen, 2021, p. 30)

Figure 17.2 was taken on a beautiful and sunny November day in Vancouver. An arch glimmering through the twin bows appears in the sky after a blissful rain shower. This poetic twin moment reminds me of my hybrid lived curriculum as a Taiwanese-Canadian and of the mythological story of Hongu Utux (Rainbow Bridge) from the Atayal people. The Atayal is one the largest Indigenous communities in Taiwan, the island where I was born and raised before I eventually immigrated to "Canada," a name given by the settler colonies. For centuries, Indigenous people in Taiwan experienced economic competition and military conflict with a series of colonizing newcomers such as Han Chinese and Japanese settlers. The colonial-settler governments forced a language shift, and cultural assimilation has resulted in varying degrees

FIGURE 6.3. Coming home and home coming. *Source*: Patricia Liu Baergen.

of loss of Indigenous language, culture, and identity. For many people in my generation, the story of the Atayal's Hongu Utux was not known to us since it was not a part of the school curriculum. In the textbook, I only learned that there are "nine tribes of Indigenous people in Taiwan." The context of "Who are the Indigenous people on and from this land? What are their cultural heritages?" is concealed under the political agenda of the colonial government.

It was not until many years later that I learned a little bit more about the Atayal story from my father, a historian scholar. The traditional territory of the Atayal lies in the central mountain range in northern Taiwan, between 500 and 2,500 metres above sea level. The Atayal see themselves as the protectors of Taiwan's central and northern mountain ranges with a fierce nature, martial tradition, and strong spiritual beliefs. Historically, they are known for their proud, unyielding spirit. During the Japanese colonialization of Taiwan, the Atayal fought against the Japanese and gained the name of "the fierce ones." The Atayal have a strong spiritual belief that became the ethical code of conduct that guides their life, one that includes the legend of the Rainbow Bridge.*

Atayal people believe that life does not end on Earth and that to reach the world of eternal life they must cross the Rainbow Bridge—the only path on which they can return "home" to be reunited with their ancestors. Returning home, for the Atayal, is a twin moment of their earthly unfolding and heavenly being. The Rainbow Bridge stands tall and majestic, touches the sky, and shines brightly in the seven colours of the rainbow, arching across the horizon. Below the Rainbow Bridge lies a deep, daunting abyss; a roaring, foaming river rapidly runs through its course, a place filled with crocodiles and giant pythons. At the head of the bridge abides

---

* For information about the mythology of the Atayal Rainbow Bridge and their heritage, I relied on an unpublished thesis by Jiang (2001).

a room where the Atayal peoples' souls wait to cross the Rainbow Bridge. Only the ethical men who know how to hunt and the righteous women who know how to weave, having fulfilled their social responsibilities, will be able to cross the Rainbow Bridge to return home and unite with their ancestors. Others will fall off the bridge into the abyss. The Atayal also believe that a woman's customary facial tattoos (黥面) of the mythological signs and symbols serve as a "permit" to pass across the Rainbow Bridge.

The Atayal also weave these mythological signs and symbols into textile patterns. Atayal women traditionally used horizontal strap looms (*wubun*) for weaving with naturally dyed plants such as ramie. Later, with the increased trading between the Han Chinese and the Japanese settlers, the Atayal wove hand-coloured cotton threads into their textiles. Even today, weaving is an important skill for Atayal women and only the ones who master the skill can be considered a *Nelin na tayan* (a true Atayal woman). The social status of an Atayal woman is still determined by her weaving skills. The skills and patterns can only be passed on from mother to daughter, and the patterns vary from one household to another. The juxtaposition of the signs and symbols in the patterns reveal familial stories. A piece of Atayal textile whispers the historical teaching of a familial, lived curriculum.

In the Atayal culture, which has no written language, weaving is a way of telling the lived stories of the ancestors, with ancestral spirit worship being the theme of weaving design. In ancient times, to record the path where the ancestors traversed, the people expressed the historical inheritance and the significance of these mythological implications in the symbols woven through their fine patterns. *Dowrig*, or diamond-shaped patterns, are frequently found in Atayal textile; in the Atayal language, *dowrig* means "the ancestors' eyes;" the Atayal believe that wearing their ancestors' eyes will bring them protection.

Despite the Atayal having lived through Japanese colonialism (from 1895 to 1945) and Han Chinese settlement (from 1945 to the present day), they have preserved the culture of weaving. The Atayal's textiles, a lived curriculum, serve as important historical artifacts about their ancestral teachings. In turn, for Atayal women, weaving is not only a skill that can meet the practical needs of their family. It is a way of life to access a wholesome Atayal world, physically and spiritually. Weaving the vibrant, colourful threads with the traditional horizontal strap looms, wubun, Atayal women build and find their own way to the Rainbow Bridge through the creation of a textile—a twin moment of lived curriculum transcending curriculum space that embodies their physical and spiritual beings coming home.

Today, most of the Atayal remain living harmoniously with the environment on their ancestral territories. Wulai (烏來), neighbouring the capital city, Taipei, is one of the territories with a large Atayal community in the northern part of Taiwan. Popular for its hot springs, Wulai, meaning "hot springs," is known for its preserved natural landscape. The Atayal believe that the origin of the name Wulai can be traced back three hundred years when, one day, Atayal warriors hunted and tracked their prey to this place. From a distance, the warriors saw smoking hot water gushing out from a crevice of the river valley. The warriors shouted *ulay kilux*! *Kilux* in the Atayal language means "hot," and *ulay* means "spring." Hence its name, Wulai. Since its discovery, the Atayal people have used the riverbed of the hot springs on both sides of the river as their natural bathing place. Wulai is also known for its beauty, with a waterfall tumbling over rocks feeding into an emerald-coloured lake, amid the mountains, forest trails, and the pecking and croaking of woodpeckers and frogs. A wooden suspension bridge, built originally by the Atayal, hangs poetically over the lake, connecting the community trails to the access roads.

From Taipei, where my parents have lived most of their life, Wulai is just a 40-minute drive along mountainous roads. Along with these stories of the Atayal people that my father shared with me when he took me hiking the trails in Wulai, he shared how Wulai was an all-time favourite place of his, a place where he first dated my mother. Despite the colonial settlers keeping the Indigenous name of this place, the narratives of the Atayal communities and their lived stories about colonialism remain a "historic hollow" (Ng-A-Fook, 2011, p. 322) in the school curriculum, at least when I studied in Taiwan.

When I was growing up in Taiwan, my lived curriculum resided, juxtaposed, in between the historic hollow in the school curriculum of Indigenous peoples' stories and the diasporic curriculum of my parents. Their feelings of being on the land of "others" and their longing for belonging further complicated my understanding of my lived curriculum. My parents, who were Han settlers, individually retreated to Taiwan from China in 1949 along with the Kuomintang-led government (國民黨). During the civil war (國共戰爭) between the Communist party (共產黨) and the Kuomintang (國民黨), or Nationalist Party, the Communists gained control of mainland China and established the People's Republic of China (PRC) in 1949, forcing the leaders of the Republic of China (ROC) to retreat to the island of Taiwan. Starting in the 1950s, a lasting political and military standoff between the countries on either side of the Taiwan Strait ensued, with the ROC in Taiwan and the PRC in mainland China both officially claiming to be the legitimate government of China. After the 1958

Taiwan Strait Crisis, both parties tacitly ceased fire in 1979. However, no armistice or peace treaty has ever been signed.

My mother came to Taiwan with her family on a relatively uneventful trip. My father came to Taiwan alone with his schoolmates and teachers. His diasporic curriculum started on a gloomy rainy day in Beijing when, in a Beijing high school, the principal announced to the students, teachers, and administrators that the military troops were approaching the periphery of the school district. The whole school decided to evacuate east toward the coastline where the safe zone was. My father, who had decided to continue his schooling, quickly returned home to inform his parents about his decision, not realizing that it was their last farewell. My father was later compelled to escape to Taiwan with his classmates and teachers. After a long journey by foot, by train, and by boat, he finally arrived in the Keelung Harbour, near the capital city of Taipei. My father could only locate eight of his classmates.

Life during the post-war years was not easy, especially for a diasporic young man who left home and lived alone in a new land, culture, language, and climate. He went from four distinct seasons to one warm, humid spring-like season, from eating flour-based staple foods to rice, from speaking Mandarin to being surrounded by the Minnan dialect (閩南語). A feeling of estrangement accompanied his maturation as a young man. Perhaps these momentous life events of his diasporic curriculum left an imprint on him. Despite his establishment of a happy, secure, and comfortable home in Taiwan for himself and his family and a well-respected career, my father always longed to return "home" to China. He lived in this state like a twin moment of dwelling in between two places, two lived curricula, until the end of his life.

It was 2020, January 20, on the first day of the Chinese New Year, when I learned that my father was admitted to the hospital intensive care unit for Parkinson's-related complications in his old age. Just a few days earlier, I had spoken to him on the phone, a routine that we had established after I left home almost 20 years ago, and now he was in a coma, breathing on life support. I was very close to my father. Every weekend, my father expected my call, and after one or two rings, I knew he would pick up the phone. We talked about things that had happened in the past week as if I had never left home and moved 6,000 miles away. My father watched the news faithfully and paid special attention to the weather forecast in my location. He often opened the conversations with weather-related comments, like "The weather has been nice in Vancouver." My father, also a university professor, supported my idea of "altering my path" to enter a PhD program later in life. During our weekly phone conversations, we would talk about things inside and outside the academic world. He was a great advisor throughout my life. His experience of working in academia and his wise words, like the bright North Star, had accompanied me through some dark woods. In the last few years, Parkinson's disease had started impacting his speech ability; it became my turn to ask him what his days were like during the week. Often, I could tell from his refreshing voice that he had been out and about during the week, gone to restaurants with his friends or had coffee with his previous colleagues or students in his/our favourite place—Wulai. He also liked to end our conversation with weather comments like, "It is getting colder there, so dress warmly." Monitoring the weather conditions 6,000 miles away and slipping in comments through a seemingly mundane routine was his way of expressing love. In retrospect, my father placed me and my whereabouts in his daily thoughts.

My father loved outdoor activities. Before I went to high school, during the days in the long summer vacation when my mother had to work, my father would take me to his campus, or to swimming lessons, camping, hiking, restaurants. We both enjoyed hiking and liked to "reward" ourselves with a meal or an afternoon tea after our hiking. We hiked many national park trails and, of course, those scenic trails in Wulai. Every spring, we would pay our visit to the breathtaking cherry blossoms along the trails in Wulai. After the fresh air and physical workout, we would find an outdoor hot spring to relax. I was always greedy for the warm sensation of soaking myself in the light-emerald spring water and would not get out until all my fingers wrinkled. Usually, by this time, we were very hungry, and "restaurant hunting" would extend our trip. This one-day trip became a spring ritual between us, and it lasted for years, until I left home for Europe and then Canada.

During my January 2020 visit to Taipei, while the whole city was decorated with bright red in celebration of the new year, I sat quietly beside my father's bed in the ICU. Quietly the white curtain was pulled around us. In the moment of silent space, I closed my eyes and meandered with my father again on the Wulai trails. The vivid pink and red cherry flowers blossomed around us, and the eggy odour of sulphur surrounded us. The spring, the wrinkled fingers, and the countless weekly conversations flashbacked like scene by scene in a movie—a lived curriculum that spoke the place pedagogy. After softly chanting the Amitabha* mantra for him, a

---

* Amitabha, the Buddha of Eternal Life, is also known as Amitayus, one of the five Cosmic Buddhas of Esoteric Buddhism. It is believed by the Buddhists that chanting the Amitabha mantra upon death can help the dying person to be reborn on the Western Pure Land.

sense of peaceful tranquillity emerged, and I whispered in his ears, "I love you, Dad, and I will see you at home, in Pure Land."*

Through the unceasing love from my father, in this final moment of our "last conversation" on earth, I experienced the transcendent meaning of home that went beyond my hybrid physical lived curriculum between Taiwan and Canada. In the twin moment in between earthly and transcendent curriculum space, I heard my Amitabha chanting merging with the sound of the Atayal women's wubun. In the twin moment in between earthly and transcendent curriculum space, I see my white prayer mala emerging into the beaming seven colours of the Atayal's Rainbow Bridge. In the twin moment in between earthly and transcendent curriculum space, the meaning of home attuned my awareness and understanding of my lived, unfolding curriculum in a fluid continuation, provoking my understanding of the operatic truth of homecoming, which goes beyond the limitations of curriculum-as-plan and the differences in the earthly lived curriculum to a transcendent curriculum place where my heart belongs. In the twin moment in between earthly and transcendent curriculum space, I see the possibility of understanding Donald's call: "How can we be simultaneously different and related?"

Epic Two: Canada, Ottawa, and Kamloops

> By probing the narratives of personhood as self-engaged with surrounding circumstances and questing and questioning for deeper meaning in the affairs of life, a situated, biographical understanding emerges through the composition of the enchanting discourse of culture, history, place, politics, class, gender, the way of knowing and the greater social welfare. (Liu Baergen, 2021, p. 30)

Little Shuswap Lake is on the Thompson River basin in Kamloops and on the ancestral land of the Little Shuswap, hence the name. Originally this land was known as Skwlāx. The colonial settlers could not say the Shuswap name, so it is known today as Squilax. Skwlāx in the Shuswap language means "black bear."

As I sit in my east-facing house in Kamloops, the morning sun shines through the window, spreading its gentle warmth over me. On the floor

---

* Pure Land, also known as Sukhavati or the Western Pure Land of Amitabha, is the paradise of Amitabha, who sits there enthroned beneath a flowering tree festooned with strands of jewels and auspicious symbols.

FIGURE 6.4. Kamloops.
Source: Patricia Liu Baergen.

beside me is Chloe, my eight-year-old Golden Retriever, comfortably basking in the sunlight. Her fur sparkles and reflects in the sunlight. Sipping a cup of Taiwanese high mountain tea, with its pear blossom fragrance and an ancient forest aroma, I take a moment to appreciate the tranquillity of the place I presently call home. A place where my husband and I have chosen to inhabit as a settler family—on the traditional ancestral land of the Tk'emlúps te Secwépemc. Home to Secwépemc for centuries.

I immigrated to Canada in autumn 2004, landing in Ottawa, Ontario, where I resided with my husband for eight years. Ottawa, which is on the traditional ancestral land of the Anishinabek, is the colonial capital city of Canada. Two rivers running through Ottawa. One is the Kichi Sibi, as named by the Anishinabek, called by settlers the Ottawa River. The other river's Anishinaabemowin name is the Pasapkedjinawong, meaning "the river that passes between the rocks"; it is now called the Rideau River. The city was named Ottawa by settlers in 1855, a name derived from the Anishinaabemowin word *adawe*, meaning "to trade." The Anishinabek people hunted, fished, and traded goods. I knew very little about the historic narratives of the Anishinabek in my first few years in Ottawa. Rather, perhaps, like many people across Canada and overseas who visit the city every year, I knew all about the Rideau Canal, the Ottawa River, and Parliament Hill and its buildings with their Gothic revival suite of

architectural elements. The official residence of the colonial prime minister of Canada, a limestone-clad mansion, stands on the south bank of
the Kichi Sibi, where I could not miss it every time I rowed past.

With these historical sites of colonialism, I was learning the history of Canada through a hidden curriculum that is fully subscribed to a
colonial political agenda drawn up by the "myth-makers of the late nine-
teenth century [who were] busy writing out Canada's past and writing in
the glory of the British Empire and British" (Ralston Saul, 2008, p. 12).
Before I became a Canadian citizen, I was required to take a test on my
"knowledge" of Canada. Reading the study guide *Discover Canada: The
Rights and Responsibilities of Citizenship*, I found it mainly emphasized the
French and British colonial settlement. The images of the Royal Canadian
Mounted Police, forts, railroads, and fur trade were portrayed as signifi-
cant Canadian facets of history. On the day of taking the oath to become a
Canadian citizen, I swore that:

> From this day forward, I pledge my loyalty and allegiance to Canada and
> Her Majesty Elizabeth the Second, Queen of Canada. I promise to respect
> our country's rights and freedoms, to uphold our democratic values,
> to faithfully observe our laws and fulfill my duties and obligations as a
> Canadian citizen. (Canadian Citizenship, 2022)

On this day, I become a foreign-born Canadian with dual citizenship
(Republic of China and Canada). Within this colonial narrative of the
binary of national identity, I first learned how to become a Canadian citizen.

Not until I entered graduate school at the University of Ottawa, then
later the University of British Columbia, did I learn of the colonial curriculum. I was immersed in the readings from various Canadian scholars' works, such as Dwayne Donald's (2009) call to educators to attend to
the ethical relationality of place, Cynthia Chambers's (1994, 1999, 2003,
2008) works on the topography for Canadian curriculum theory, Nicholas
Ng-A-Fook's works (2012, 2013, 2014) on the provocation of the "idea" of
Canadian curriculum studies, Timothy Stanley's (2009) work on the banality of colonialism. Then I continued my studies with Ted Tetsuo Aoki's cri-
tiques (1986b/2005) on the binary of dualism embedded in identity politics,
and William Pinar's (2011) work on nationalism and Canadian identity. I
was provoked to reconsider my immigrant settler's colonial identity. These
provocations and disruptions allowed me to examine my own assumptions,
and I came to understand that my self-formation as a Canadian citizen
had occurred under the influence of the historical discursive formations of

British and French colonialism. Furthermore, the "museum approach," in understanding the notion of identity and belonging as a uniform, unexamined concept that ignores the complexity of the lived curriculum of place stories and the multifaceted, intertwined process of social conditioning and self-engagement, is the root problem.

In retrospect, I also realized that the content of the study guide, *Discover Canada: The Rights and Responsibilities of Citizenship*, and the oath I took, was "fully circumscribed by colonial frontier logics" (Donald, 2009, 2012a, 2012b, 2016). It emphasized the power, control, and exploitation of resources on this Indigenous ancestral land. Furthermore, the Indigenous world view and the historic narratives of the exploitation of the Chinese immigrant railroad labourers had been eclipsed under the shadow of such colonial frontier logic. To further continue questioning and examining my assumptions and to explore the possibilities in understanding curriculum, as Pinar (2012) described, as a non-static form which pays attention to the alterity and particularity in subjectivity and Aoki's (1986b/2005) notion of curriculum-as-live(d) that directs and attunes educators to the pedagogical significance of the lived experiences of the teachers and students, in 2012 we moved to Vancouver, British Columbia, for my doctoral studies at the University of British Columbia, which is situated on the ancestral land and unceded territory of the xʷməθkʷəy̓əm (Musqueam) First Nation. During the years of my doctoral research, we eventually inhabited a settlement in Tsawwassen, on ancestral Tsawwassen First Nation land. From there, we moved to Kamloops, British Columbia, where I became a faculty member at Thompson Rivers University. The Thompson Rivers University (TRU) campuses are on the traditional lands of the Tk'emlúps te Secwépemc and the T'exelc within Secwepemcúlecw, the traditional and unceded territory of the Secwépemc. The Secwépemc people have been living on this land for thousands of years and today are a nation of 17 bands.

From my office window on campus, I have a magnificent view of the North and South Thompson Rivers winding through the valley. In the far distance, I can see the snow capping the mountains. Reflecting on my own lived curriculum of becoming a Taiwanese-Canadian, I see it as a journey of decolonizing an immigrant-settler curriculum that was embedded in the colonial-settler ideology. To reflect on this internal process of decolonizing an immigrant settler's lived curriculum, at the beginning of the semester, in each of my classes, I always make my land acknowledgement, saying "I share knowledge, teaching, learning, and research on the ancestral and unceded land of the Tk'emlúps te Secwépemc, I recognize that this territory has always been a place of teaching, learning and research by the

Secwépemc who were here before us for many centuries." Not only that; I also share my own lived stories of decolonizing my immigrant-settler curriculum. For me, it is a doubled acknowledgement that reflects my appreciation of the land and the people who were here before us and are still here today. It also serves as a renewed oath that I wish I could have said on the day I became a Canadian citizen.

To further engage decolonize my lived curriculum, in the winter semester of 2022, I joined a course offered to faculty members/administrators of the TRU School of Education. The course was led by Garry Gottfriedson, a poet and a teacher from Secwépemc First Nation. In the dark, cold wintertime, we met bi-weekly in the evenings, outside our regular working time. During three months, we learned a wide-ranging selection of curricula comprising the mystic stories of the Secwépemc, the Secwépemc language, and some awkward truths. Often, we engaged in difficult conversations initiated by Garry or by one of us. In this small group, we were settlers and immigrant-settlers of British, Colombian, French, German, Iranian, and Taiwanese backgrounds. We shared our lived curriculum of teaching and researching and reflected on our own value-laden assumptions and world views. While listening to others' stories, I momentarily experienced what Donald (2009) described as the temporality of ethical relationality as "be[ing] simultaneously different and related" (xvii).

At the end of this course, it was almost springtime, and the course organizer proposed we have a two-day retreat at the Quaaout Lodge by Little Shuswap Lake. Quaaout means "when the sun's rays first hit the water" in Secwepemctsín. On this land of the Great Spirit, I received teachings from three Indigenous Elders—knowledge holders. In the morning, Elder Mike opened the day with his speech of gratitude to the land, the food, the sun, the moon, and Mother Earth. Then followed the teachings of Elders Minnie and Flora. I was mesmerized by their vividly told stories. I laughed with them at their jokes and happy moments in life. I cried with their tearful experiences of loss, separation, and anxiety, which resulted from colonial-settler discrimination. Lunchtime arrived unexpectedly for me because the morning had slipped away. In the afternoon, the Elders, Garry, and another Indigenous faculty member joined us in workshop stations. We took turns sitting with each of them individually to ask questions. In this rare opportunity, I felt the grounding energy of Elder Mike, the mother-like warmth of Elder Minnie, and the kindred spirit of Elder Flora. Surrounded by the energies of these Elders, I dwelt poetically on the wisdom that unfolded through the found prose of Elders' in-the-world-being.

Now, I invite you to dwell with me and contemplate the question that Donald asked: "How can we be simultaneously different and related?"

Gratitude*

Five hundred years ago, people were happy
Gratitude was a part of our culture
To the water, we drink
To the food, we eat
To the language, we speak
To the life giver
Sun
Rising and shining on the planets
Nourishing the food on the table
All from Mother Earth
Gratitude building the shape of our prayers
In our spirit as our medicine
Since the time of creation
Until the seventh generation
The western culture came
Big machine, empire building
Evil worship of territories and oppressed the people
Then
Comes to the resistance of the Mother Earth
Power, control, and exploitation of resources
Who is the uncivilized?!
Truth is
You cannot lie to your children about the future
If you do the proper research
Putting resources back to human being
The meaning of reconciliation
I am telling you the stories of mine
The stories of Truth
What are yours?

* * *

---

*   This is a found poem created from the teaching of Secwépemc Elder Mike.

In 1958
Salmon was so much
In 2022
They aren't coming back
Gold is gone
Digging deep into Mother Earth for energy resources
What is next?
When the resources are gone
What do we do?
We struggle so hard now on this land

* * *

Museum approach
They put things in
the windows
People come and see
Windows after windows
This is what Indians used to do and live
They call this place a museum
I am sitting right here
Why don't you talk to me?
I will tell you the stories
I will tell you the truth
The stories that you do not lie to our children about the future
Elders are gathering here for our children
Elders are the PhD in our higher education
That is the end of our copyright!

* * *

Circle of life
Creator of the Sun radiant, the male energy circle
Protect the circle of knowing Elders
Female energy of Mother Earth
Circle around our children in the inner layer
This is the circle of life
This is the order we did things

They took the inner circle out
Send our children to residential schools
The circle system collapsed
We can't continue lying to our children
Addiction, homeless
Not an intellectual thing
But our reality
Trauma, tortures and humiliations
Not a joke to tell
But that's what they do to us
Little Joe did not want to pee in bed
Little Joe was tied down on the bed
We can't continue lying to our children
It is time to heal
It is time to heal

* * *

Eagle as Conduit and
Nature as Yourself
Butterfly, Sun
When the sun is the equator, it becomes with butterfly
The nudges in the tree in finding your way home
Eagles as conduit
They know what to do with their life
The four-legged know what to do with their life
How about us?
Do we put happiness to our food?
When you wake up
You should think about these things
I am the smartest one in Grade Two for eight years
There is no such thing as a Canadian language
They are kind of mixed-up people and language
We are trying to help them to find their way home
Nature as yourself
Body, Mind, Spirit

Unity of Freedom and Survival

Introduce yourself in your language
So the ancestorial spirit will help you
Here is where I begin
Teaching my language
The Elders come and speak in their language all day
Start with two
Then four
The room becomes too small
When we teach
There are no books
We never have books
Kids have to make their books
Go outside! dig the fruits, peel the birch bark and find fish and deer
I never went to school
My brothers and sisters went to the residential schools
I envy them for going to schools
Until
I see their bruised swollen hands
My mother told me not to speak our language in school
A girl told on us
While we spoke outside the washroom
I quit the school
Back on my grandfather's field, garden, and berry bushes
Horse riding, swimming, fishing and berry picking
Those are the best days
Out there in the land
Giggling with our grandparents in our language
Unity
I feel
Our parents never worry about us
They taught us what to eat in forest
They don't worry if we didn't come back for supper
They know we will survive
We live in unity with land
Now
Berry picking places are all gone
Canning factories dry up our berries
Hunting places are blocked

People call cops on us if we enter
We found berry bushes
With big sign "Sprayed, Poison!"
Plants turned brown
Now people talk about unity
They stayed a week indoor talking
We just go out hunting, riding, climbing and swimming
Freedom of living with survival skills
On this land
Is
Unity
Is
Home

A Lingering Epic: Past, Present, and Future— A Circle by the Fire at Cyistn

> The environment ceases to be environment, and in its place comes into being a pedagogical situation, a lived situation pregnantly alive in the presence of people. (Aoki, 1986b/1991/2005, p. 159)

The two-day retreat slipped away quickly. At the last moment, we were invited by the Elders to sit in a circle by the fire in the cyistn—a traditional Shuswap winter home. A cyistn is built half into the ground and half out of the ground with logs, tule, dirt, and grass to protect the people from the harsh winter weather. The sturdy cyistn is warm, with a fire pit in the centre and an opening on the top. The equivalent English version of the keekwillie would be "pit house." After settling in the keekwillie by the fire, we all sat quietly, listening to narratives of the non-living curriculum of the rocks by the fire and the logs, tule, dirt and grass in the cyistn, a lived curriculum merged with a transcendent curriculum space. Indigenous chanting broke the silence, and then a Spanish song followed, sung by one of our colleagues. We took turns expressing our sincere gratitude for the medicine we received from the Elders' teaching and the historical narratives of the land. At this moment, I seemed to understand Elder Flora's teaching, "On this land is unity, is home—a medicine of the heart." While the voices of three Elders telling their lived place stories, the tears, and the laughter were lingering in my mind, Donald's call for educator attention surfaced again: "How can we be simultaneously different and related?"

FIGURE 6.5. The circle by the fire.
Source: Patricia Liu Baergen.

Perhaps, dwelling poetically in between our place stories as a site of clearing—as a curriculum-as-lived that "mirrors earth, sky, mortals, and divinity" (Heidegger, 1975, in Liu Baergen, 2018, p. 149) in our longing to be together—we can "hear the rhythmic measure of the earth, our place of dwelling, where its earthy humus provides nurturance to new meanings of humiliation that are springing forth," while "lingering in this space of lived tensionality of [our] difference[s]" (Aoki, 1993/2005, p. 300). Perhaps, living in tensionality of differences is a "mode of being, of living simultaneously with limitations and with open-ness, but also that this openness harbours within it risks and possibilities as we quest for a change from the *is* to the *not yet*" (Aoki, 1986b/1991/2005, p. 164). Dwelling poetically in between our place stories is not so much "the elimination of the differences, but, more so, the attunement of the quality of the tensionality of differences that makes a difference" (Aoki, 1987/2005, p. 354).

To engage with such dwelling is not a romanticized worship of the stories nor a denigrated difference of ideologies. Rather, it is an active engagement with the self and with the public in a complicated conversation. Such conversation, I believe, should be a labour of seeking a layered understanding of how one's own situated, lived curriculum is embedded in a larger socio-cultural and political context. This requires not only recognizing the longstanding history, languages, wisdom, and traditions that came before the settlers, but also requires one to seek an understanding of one's place within this colonial history—the exploitation of power, land, resources, and the binary of dualism embedded in identity politics. I believe that a part of such conversation should not only engage with the past as colonial history but also examine colonialism as a historical present in which we live. As an immigrant settler, educator, and curriculum theorist, it is important for me to develop mindfulness of my present participation to continue engaging in this challenging but necessary conversation. It is, for me, a learning journey of decolonization through building relationships with the ancestral land of the Indigenous people.

In turn, I suggest that belonging does not mean paying homage to sameness. Rather, dwelling where we are on this Indigenous ancestral land and listening to each other's stories in different languages, cultures, and beliefs is an extension of receiving medicine from the land to give to each other. I hope that we can attune to one another, catch sight or hear the sound of our being in our essential togetherness that rests not in sameness but as human dwelling in this place of belonging. Through dwelling in between the juxtaposition of my own place stories and the Indigenous place stories as lived curricula, I hope to explore curriculum as a "narrative inquiry of lived experiences that can disclose the existential texture of the beings that teachers and students come to be" (Liu Baergen, 2021, p. 78). Through this reflective process of examining how social conditioning and self-engagement intertwine, I hope to first help myself, as an immigrant/settler/educator/curriculum theorist, never to lose sight that "beneath all our feet is land which has existed and does exist first of all in relation to Indigenous people" (Haig-Brown, 2009, p. 15). Then, to engage further this complicated conversation in the classroom to build "student capacity for intercultural understanding, empathy, and mutual respect" (Call to Action 63, Truth and Reconciliation Commission of Canada, 2015, p. 7).

Also, through juxtaposing my autobiographical narratives with three Indigenous Elders' place stories, poetry, and visual art as a conceptual and methodological approach, I hope to provide some insight into ways to explore curriculum as an experience of poetic dwelling in between place stories. By sharing my lived stories and my own situatedness in the process of decolonizing an immigrant settler's lived curriculum, I hope to further call educators' attention to the notion of understanding as a mode of being in response to Donald's question: "How can we be simultaneously different and related?" Lastly, I suggest that exploring curriculum as an experience of poetic dwelling may help bring an authentic voice to the surface. Such poetic dwelling on one's lived curriculum evokes inner feelings, liberating the untold truth from momentous life events and transforming them into precious pedagogical moments that question the historical present and that juxtapose history, society, and subjectivity. In turn, curriculum becomes an inquiry that dwells in between one's own lived place stories.

References

Aoki, T. T. (1978/1980/2005). Toward curriculum inquiry in a new key. In Pinar, W. F., & Irwin, R. L. (Eds.), *Curriculum in a new key: The collected works of Ted T. Aoki* (pp. 89–110). Lawrence Erlbaum Associates.

Aoki, T. T. (1979/2005). Reflections of a Japanese Canadian teacher experiencing ethnicity. In Pinar, W. F., & Irwin, R. L. (Eds.), *Curriculum in a new key: The collected works of Ted T. Aoki* (pp. 333–348). Lawrence Erlbaum Associates.

Aoki, T. T. (1986a/1991/2005). Signs of vitality in curriculum scholarship. In Pinar, W. F., & Irwin, R. L. (Eds.), *Curriculum in a new key: The collected works of Ted T. Aoki* (pp. 229–234). Lawrence Erlbaum Associates.

Aoki, T. T. (1986b/1991/2005). Teaching as indwelling between two curriculum worlds. In Pinar, W. F., & Irwin, R. L. (Eds.), *Curriculum in a new key: The collected works of Ted T. Aoki* (pp. 159–165). Lawrence Erlbaum Associates.

Aoki, T. T. (1987/2005). Revisiting the notions of leadership and identity. In Pinar, W. F., & Irwin, R. L. (Eds.), *Curriculum in a new key: The collected works of Ted T. Aoki* (pp. 349–355). Lawrence Erlbaum Associates.

Aoki, T. T. (1993/2005). Humiliating the Cartesian Ego. In Pinar, W. F., & Irwin, R. L. (Eds.), *Curriculum in a new key: The collected works of Ted T. Aoki* (pp. 291–301). Lawrence Erlbaum Associates.

Canadian Citizenship (2022). *Oath of Canada citizenship.* https://www.edu.gov. mb.ca/k12/cur/socstud/foundation_gr9/blms/9-2-4e.pdf

Chambers, C. (1994). Looking for a home: A work in progress. *Frontiers: A Journal of Woman Studies,* 15(2), 23–50.

Chambers, C. (1999). A topography for Canadian curriculum theory. *Canadian Journal of Education,* 24(2), 137–150.

Chambers, C. (2003). "As Canadian as possible under the circumstances": A view of contemporary curriculum discourses in Canada. In Pinar, W. F. (Ed.), *International handbook of curriculum research* (pp. 221–252). Lawrence Erlbaum Associates.

Chambers, C. (2008). Where are we? Finding common ground in a curriculum of place. *Journal of the Canadian Association for Curriculum Studies,* 6(2), 113–128.

Donald, D. (2009). A question. In Hasebe-Ludt, E. Chambers, C., & Leggo, C., *Life writing and literary métissage as an ethos for our times* (p. xvi). Peter Lang.

Donald, D. (2012a). Forts, colonial frontier logics, and aboriginal-Canadian relations: Imagining decolonizing educational philosophies in Canadian contexts. In Abdi, A. (Ed.), *Decolonizing Philosophies of Education* (pp. 91–111). Sense Publishers.

Donald, D. (2012b). Forts, curriculum, and ethical relationality. In Ng-A-Fook, N., & Rottmann, J. (Eds.), *Reconsidering Canadian curriculum studies—provoking historical, present, and future perspectives* (pp. 39–46). Palgrave Macmillan.

Donald, D. (2016). From what dopes ethical relationality flow? An "Indian" act in three artifacts. In Seidel, J., & Jardine, D., W., *The Ecological heart of teaching: Radical tales of refuges and renewal for classrooms and communities* (pp. 10–16). Peter Lang.

Jiang, W. (2001). 傳承.變奏與斷列: 以當代太魯閣族女性之織布文化為例. 碩士論文, 國立東華大學 [Heritage, variation and fragmentation: A study of the contemporary Atayal women's weaving culture] [Unpublished doctoral thesis]. National Dong Hwa University.

Haig-Brown, C. (2009). Decolonizing diaspora: Whose traditional lad are we on? *Cultural and Pedagogical Inquiry*, 1(1), 4–21.

Heidegger, M. (1975). *Poetry, language, thought* (A. Hofstadter, Trans.). Harper & Row.

Liu Baergen, P. (2018). Theorizing as poetic dwelling: An intellectual link between Ted Aoki and Martin Heidegger. In Hasebe-Ludt, E., & Leggo, C. (Eds.), *Canadian curriculum studies: A métissage of inspiration/imagination/interconnection* (pp. 141–150). Canadian Scholars.

Liu Baergen, P. (2021). *Tracing Ted T. Aoki's Intellectual Formation: Understanding Historical, Societal, and Phenomenological Influences*. Routledge, Taylor & Francis Group.

Ng-A-Fook, N. (2011). Decolonizing narrative strands of our eco-civic responsibilities: Curriculum, social, action and indigenous communities. In Stanley, W., & Young, K. (Eds.), *Contemporary Studies in Canadian Curriculum* (pp. 313–342). Brush Education.

Ng-A-Fook, N. (2013). Contemplating a Canadian curriculum theory project: Currere, Denkbild, and intellectual genealogies. In Hurren, W., & Hasebe-Ludt, E. (Eds.), *Contemplating curriculum: Genealogies/times/places* (pp. 172–182). Routledge.

Ng-A-Fook, N. (2014). Provoking the very "idea" of Canadian curriculum studies as a counterpointed composition. *Journal of the Canadian Association for Curriculum Studies*, 12(1), 10–69.

Ng-A-Fook, N., & Rottmann, J. (Eds.). (2012). *Reconsidering Canadian curriculum studies—provoking historical, present, and future perspectives*. Palgrave Macmillan.

Pinar, W. F. (2011). Nationalism, anti-Americanism, Canadian identity. In Yates, L., & Grumet, M. (Eds.), *World yearbook of education 2011: Curriculum in today's world*, (pp. 31–41). Routledge.

Pinar, W. F. (2012). *What is curriculum theory?* (2nd ed.). Routledge.

Pinar, W. F., & Reynolds, W. M. (Eds.). (1992). *Understanding curriculum as phenomenological and deconstructed text*. Teachers College Press.

Pinar, W. F., Reynolds, W. M., Slattery, P., & Toubman, P. M. (1995). *Understanding curriculum*. Peter Lang.

Ralston Saul, J. (2008). *A fair country: Telling truths about Canada*. Penguin Canada.

Stanley, T. (2009). The banality of colonialism: Encountering artifacts of genocide and white supremacy in Vancouver today. In Steinberg, S. (Ed.), *Diversity and multiculturalism*, pp. 143–159. Peter Lang.

Truth and Reconciliation Commission of Canada. (2015). *Truth and Reconciliation Commission of Canada: Calls to Action.* https://ehprnh2mwo3.exactdn.com/wp-content/uploads/2021/01/Calls_to_Action_English2.pdf

Afterword

Tina Matthew

Weyt-kp xwexwéytep Tina Matthew *ren skwekwst te* Simpcw *re st'7é7kwen*. My *kíʔce* (mom) is Geraldine Sampson from Neskonlith and her mom is Mary Allen from Neskonlith, and her dad is Joe Sampson from Adams Lake Indian Band. My *qéʔtse* (dad) is Ron Matthew from Simpcw, his mom is Delores Jules from Skeetchestn, and his dad is Wilfred Matthew from Simpcw First Nation. I have deep family ties through Secwepemcúĺecw and many *Ḱwséltkten* throughout the nation.

I would like to thank the Tk'emlúps te Secwépemc for allowing us to be guests in their beautiful territory and acknowledge our Elders, leaders, and those who have gone before us into the spirit world. I would like to say *kukwstsétsemc* (thank you) for the teachings and support that have brought us all here today.

Thompson Rivers University's (TRU) Kamloops campus, our first house, is on the traditional territory of the Tk'emlúps te Secwépemc, and our second house is located on the territory of the T'exelc (Williams Lake First Nation), host of the TRU Williams Lake campus. Both TRU campuses are located in the heart of Secwepemcúĺecw, the traditional and unceded lands of the Secwépemc Nation. The TRU service area also includes the territories of the St'át'imc, Nlaka'pamux, Nuxalk, Tŝilhqot'in, Dakelh, and Syilx Nations.

It is an honour to be asked by Garry Gottfriedson, the TRU Secwépemc Cultural Advisor, to contribute some words for this collection, which brings together voices and thoughts from across the university. I am going to share with you my thoughts on accountability, responsibility, and action as it relates to reconciliation at TRU.

I have been giving the word "reconciliation" a great deal of thought, especially what it means to a Secwépemc woman working at TRU. Please let me be clear, I do not speak on behalf of all Indigenous people, the Secwépemc Nation, nor my community of Simpcw First Nation. These views are my own, and I am only sharing my personal thoughts and experiences at a post-secondary institution. When I returned home to Secwepemcúĺecw in 2010, I brought a variety of work experience and knowledge with me. I have been employed in the TRU Office of Indigenous Education since 2018. This office reports directly to the provost and vice-president academic, and we work closely with the deans and faculty on Indigenization by incorporating the TRC's 94 Calls to Action and the United Nations Declaration on the Rights of Indigenous Peoples at all levels of the university. We also act as a liaison between TRU and Indigenous communities for research, partnerships, and collaborations.

I have a great deal of respect for Dr. Nathan Matthew, TRU's first Secwépemc chancellor. He has created a very strong foundation for Indigenous inquiry at the university and started some important initiatives that I am happy to continue working on. During his time as executive director of the Office of Indigenous Education, he asked very important questions of the president, senior administration, and faculty about accountability and Indigenization. We are all accountable for our learning about and understanding of Secwépemc people, our hosts who have been here since time immemorial. It is all our responsibility to learn about Canada's true history, and also learn what it means to be a respectful guest in this territory. On the 1910 *Memorial to Sir Wilfrid Laurier*, the Secwépemc and Okanagan chiefs were quite clear in their message to the provincial and federal governments about our expectations of the guests in our lands:

"Thus, they commenced to enter our 'houses,' or live on our 'ranches.' With us when a person enters our house, he becomes our guest, and we must treat hi'm hospitably as long as he shows no hostile intentions. At the same time, we expect him to return to us equal treatment for what he receives" (Chiefs of the Shuswap, Okanagan and Couteau Tribes of British Columbia, 1910). A lot of learning and sharing needs to take place across Canada and especially at universities regarding reconciliation. The public and post-secondary school systems have been proactive in their efforts to Indigenize their curricula and invite Indigenous people and community members into their classrooms. This is an excellent example of empowering

Indigenous people to share our stories in meaningful and impactful ways. It is encouraging that educators are asking questions and being accountable for their own learning, as well as that of their students. Public and private industries and organizations are asking these same questions and creating meaningful learning opportunities as well. It is not up to Indigenous people to teach about who we are; it is up to every single person in this country to be accountable and responsible for their own learning about Indigenous people.

Reconciliation means many different things. I have heard it referred to in accounting terms as "balancing the books" or making things equal before we can move forward. I have also read about reconcili*action* where we are not passive receivers of information, but actively taking steps to create change in our workplace, our communities, and organizations, and challenging some of the preconceptions people may have. Reconciliation is acknowledging all parts of Canada's history, hearing firsthand accounts of how Indigenous people are striving ahead today, being a supportive ally, and taking action. Reconciliation is about having open, honest discussions with your families, community members, and colleagues. Reconciliation is attending Indigenous-hosted events, visiting local communities, and weaving Indigenous content and knowledge at all levels of your personal and work life. TRU provides many opportunities to learn and participate and we hope to see more supporters, volunteers, and allies at our events. We are all accountable and responsible for our learning as well as acting and showing support for the local Indigenous communities in any we that we can. We look forward to moving forward together in a good and respectful way.

I leave you with one question: What is your relationship with the local Indigenous people whose territory you are living and working on?

Kukwstsétsemc.

References

Chiefs of the Shuswap, Okanagan and Couteau Tribes of British Columbia. (1910). *Memorial to Sir Wilfrid Laurier, Premier of the Dominion of Canada.* In 1910 Memorial to Sir Wilfred Laurier, Qwelmínte Secwépemc. https://www.qwelminte.ca/1910-memorial-to-sir-wilfred-laurier

Contributors

This section lists the authors of the articles, stories, and poetry in alphabetical order. All participated in the rich conversations about Indigenous literature and issues with Garry Gottfriedson and/or participated in the two-day retreat that included Elders from Secwepemcúlecw and our Indigenous colleagues.

All our participants are on personal journeys of truth and reconciliation. Their contributions are all sincere representations of their journey in 2021. They have more rivers to cross, hills to climb, and issues to respectfully consider. It is with humility and recognition that change is part of the growth that they have risked that they submitted these materials that will be published long after their thinking may have evolved.

Dorothy Cucw-la7 Christian is Secwépemc and Syilx from the interior plateau regions of what is known as British Columbia. She is happy to be a good relative to her Coast Salish cousins while she lives, works, and plays on their lands. Her research centralizes land, story, cultural protocols, and how Indigenous knowledge informs and guides interrelationships with Canadian settler society. Her curiosity about how cultural knowledge influences Indigenous production practices started when she was working for the national broadcaster VisionTV to bring Indigenous stories to the screen.

Dorothy works as the associate director, Indigenous Policy and Pedagogy at Simon Fraser University. While she writes scholarly chapters and participates in community on many levels, Dorothy remains involved in the Indigenous visual storytelling culture in Canada. She serves as a board member of the Indigenous Screen Office in Toronto and curated programs for the 2018 and 2019 ImagineNATIVE film festival, the largest Indigenous film festival in the world.

Georgann Cope Watson is an Open Learning faculty member in the Faculty of Education and Social Work at Thompson Rivers University. She is invested in qualitative research methods that inquire into decolonization and reconciliation, the praxis of critical and feminist pedagogy, the pedagogy of adult education, and the pedagogy of online teaching. Current research projects include the praxis of reconcili*action*. Georgann lives, works, studies, teaches, and plays on the traditional territory of Ktunaxa First Nation.

Garry Gottfriedson is from Kamloops, BC. He is strongly rooted in his Secwépemc (Shuswap) cultural teachings. He holds a Master of Arts Education degree from Simon Fraser University. In 1987, the Naropa Institute (now University) in Boulder, Colorado, awarded a Creative Writing Scholarship to Gottfriedson for Master of Fine Arts in Creative Writing. There, he studied under Allen Ginsberg, Marianne Faithfull, and others. Gottfriedson has 12 published books. He has read from his work across Canada, the United States, South America, New Zealand, Europe, and Asia. Gottfriedson's work unapologetically unveils the truth of Canada's treatment of First Nations. His work has been anthologized and published nationally and internationally. He recently received an honorary Doctor of Laws degree from the University of Northern British Columbia.

Victoria (Tory) Handford is a professor in the Faculty of Education and Social Work at Thompson Rivers University and is currently the chair of the School of Education. Prior to moving to TRU, Tory held multiple positions in JK–12 education as a teacher, vice-principal, and principal. She has been an education officer (Leadership) for the Ontario Ministry of Education and program officer (Standards of Practice and Accreditation) for the Ontario College of Teachers. Her recent publications include a three-book series that addresses experiences of faculty in Canadian universities. Tory has also published multiple articles and chapters addressing components of school and district leadership.

Sarah Ladd is currently the administrative coordinator for the graduate programs in education at Thompson Rivers University, responsible for non-academic coordination of two programs, which have more than 500 students annually. She is regularly involved in the hiring of staff and faculty. Prior to this, she spent 14 years as a post-secondary career advisor at TRU, the University of British Columbia, the University of Calgary, and Simon Fraser University. She remains passionate about all aspects of career development and is working to learn more about how Western career models can be changed and improved to be more inclusive for newcomers and Indigenous people.

Patricia Liu Baergen is an assistant professor at Thompson Rivers University. She completed her PhD in curriculum studies at the University of British Columbia. Firmly rooted in the field of curriculum theory/izing and informed by the continental philosophy of Martin Heidegger, Patricia's research interests include curriculum studies, life history, theorizing pedagogy, and educational philosophy.

Tina Matthew is a proud Secwépemc woman and member of Simpcw First Nation located in the North Thompson Valley in the interior of BC. She is honoured to hold the position of executive director in the Office of Indigenous Education at Thompson Rivers University. Tina holds a Master of Education and an undergraduate degree from Simon Fraser University. She is an education professional with over 30 years' experience working with Indigenous communities, organizations, public and private institutions, and industry. She has particular strengths in conducting research, developing organizational processes, and connecting Indigenous people with training and collaboration opportunities. She is an active community member who always strives for self-governance and leadership for all Indigenous people through mentorship and respectful leadership.

Rod McCormick is an Indigenous health researcher and clinician. His nation is Kanien'kehá:ka (Mohawk). He lives on reserve in his partner's home community of Tk'emlúps te Secwépemc. His professional training and experience is in counselling psychology and in Indigenous mental health. He was a psychologist and counselling psychology professor at the University of British Columbia for 18 years and a professor of education at Thompson Rivers University (TRU) for the last 11 years. His research focuses on community capacity building in Indigenous mental health and research as well as the reclamation of traditional forms of healing. He has been a clinician, consultant, trainer, and researcher in Indigenous mental health for approximately 35 years. He was the lead for the BC Aboriginal Capacity and Developmental Research Environments, the BC Network Environments for Aboriginal Health Research, the Kloshe Tillicum research network, and he is currently the lead on the national/international Indigenous mentorship network Ombaashi, as well as the Knowledge Makers program and the All My Relations Research Centre at TRU.

Gloria Ramirez is a professor in the Faculty of Education and Social Work at Thompson Rivers University, where she teaches courses on language, literacy, and research methods in education. She has more than 30 years of teaching experience in K–12 and higher education in Colombia, England, and Canada. Her research examines language and literacy development across different languages, bilingual learning, and the revitalization of Indigenous languages. Specifically, she examines effective teaching strategies to accelerate language learning and reading development. She has been collaborating with Secwépemc scholars, educators, Elders, and knowledge keepers for about 12 years on initiatives to revitalize Secwepemctsín. She is currently learning Secwepemctsín as an act of decolonization.

Fred Schaub is an online learning faculty member and sessional instructor with Thompson Rivers University and a sessional instructor at Vancouver Island University. As an educational leader, Fred has worked at all levels of the K–12 public education system, including at an independent band school in British Columbia. For the last 20 years, Fred has been on a journey of learning to walk respectfully in both worlds, the Indigenous and the non-Indigenous. He has developed close relational and professional ties to Indigenous communities along the BC coast and holds the honour of being adopted into two Indigenous families. One of Fred's greatest accolades is being described as a cultural ambassador by an Indigenous Elder and Knowledge Keeper; he attempts to honour this description every day.

Bernita Weinhold-Leahy is a university instructor in the Faculty of Education and Social Work at Thompson Rivers University. Bernita worked in special education in the K–12 system for more than a decade, when she became concerned by the numbers of students suffering from mental health issues. She studied contemplative practices and became a mindfulness and compassion teacher to help students build resiliency. Her research interests relate to mindfulness and compassion toward students and teachers to encourage personal well-being and inner strength.

FIGURE 1. All of us (many participants and contributors).
Source: Victoria Handford.

Appendix 1

TABLE A1. Action Plan for Reconcili*action*

TRC Call to Action	63 iii. Building student capacity for intercultural understanding, empathy, and mutual respect 63 iv. Identifying teacher-training needs relating to the above
EDUC5041 Course Learning Outcome	Have a general understanding of how education privileges or disadvantages races, ethnicities, classes, genders, and sexual orientations, and demonstrate an understanding of how various theoretical perspectives can be applied to that study
First Peoples Principles of Learning	• Learning is holistic, reflexive, reflective, experiential, and relational (focused on connectedness, on reciprocal relationships, and a sense of place) • Learning requires exploration of one's identity
Reconcili*action*	• Include a formal statement recognizing the relationship I have to the land and acknowledging Indigenous peoples and the traditional territory I am connected to (TRU) • Challenge the dominant narratives around collective histories and challenges (UR) • Include content on IRSS, MMIWG, and Land Disputes (UR) • Critically examine colonization (UR) • Deconstruct whiteness neutrality (UR) • Take up emerging Indigenous issues as they unfold (UR) • Visit an Indigenous community (UR)
Learning Activities	• Field trip to an Indigenous community • Add learning activities for important dates: i.e., Red Dress, Orange Shirt, National Day for Truth and Reconciliation, 215 • Study the First Peoples Principles of Learning: Add an activity to honour each one • Include the Privilege Walk Lesson • Analysis of the Deficit Ideology • Continue to bring The Hidden and Null Curriculum to the forefront • Arrange seating in a circle or in circle groups

TRC Call to Action	63 iii. Building student capacity for intercultural understanding, empathy, and mutual respect
EDUC 5041 Course Learning Outcome	Be familiar with the principal scholars writing on issues relating to the intersection of education with race, ethnicity, class, gender, and sexual orientation, and demonstrate an understanding of the research methods used in the literature
First Peoples Principles of Learning	• Learning is embedded in memory, history, and story • Learning recognizes the role of Indigenous knowledge
Reconcili*action*	• Engage and attend Indigenous community events when they are open to the public (TRU) • Review course outline and scope and sequence for Indigenous content and scholars (UR) • Seek out and review the work of Indigenous scholars in the field of Education (UR)
Learning Activities and Assessments	• Review creation stories • Integrate learning activities on recognizing Colourblindness, Microaggression, Meritocracy and False Narratives • Field Trip or Virtual Field Trip to the Secwepemc Museum and Heritage Park • Complete the Diversity Wheel Learning Activity • View the Blanket Exercise Video • Complete an analysis of Jane Elliot's' Blue Eyes-Brown Eyes Experiment on Anti-Racism
TRC Call to Action	63 iv. Identifying teacher-training needs relating to the above
EDUC 5041 Course Learning Outcome	Be able to read both primary materials and secondary documents critically for issues of race, ethnicity, class, gender, sexual orientation and education
FPPL	• Learning requires exploration of one's identity • Learning involves recognizing that some knowledge is sacred and only shared with permission and/or in certain situations
Reconcili*action*	• Include Indigenous scholarly readings into the reading list (UR) • Identify existing courses within the faculty and share these with students (UR) • Integrate Story Telling as pedagogy (TRU)

Learning Activities and Assessments	• Add readings or videos of some of the principal Canadian Indigenous Scholars: Marie Batiste (2013), JoAnne Archibald (2008), Dwayne Donald (2012), Robert Joseph (2018), Thomas King (2018), Taiaiake Alfred (2021), Garry Gottfredson (2008), Ron and Marianne Ignace (2017), Arthur Manuel (1974), Michelle Pidgeon (2016), Richard Wagamese (2012) • Assign a Literature review on a topic specific to Indigenous peoples • Create a place-based learning unit • Include an assignment on critically analyzing an Indigenous based film • Final Project: Analysis of the TRC Calls to Action
TRC Call to Action	63 ii. Sharing information and best practices on teaching curriculum related to residential schools and Aboriginal history 63 iii. Building student capacity for intercultural understanding, empathy, and mutual respect 63 iv. Identifying teacher-training needs relating to the above
EDUC 5041 Course Learning Outcome	• Feel confident in succinctly and critically writing about, or otherwise depicting, issues of race, ethnicity, class, gender, sexual orientation, and education
First Peoples Principles of Learning	• Learning involves patience and time • Learning involves recognizing that some knowledge is sacred and only shared with permission and/or in certain situations
Reconcili*action*	• Include Critical Race Theory in the Curriculum • Learn basic Secwepemc or other FN language and pronounciation (TRU)
Learning Activities and Assessments	• Study the historical timeline of Indigenous North America as an analytic tool to create context • Present *21 Things you May not Know about the Indian Act* by Robert Joseph (2018) • Create a learning activity with Critical Race Theory • Have a pre and post assessment learning activity on Indigenous history in Canada • Include a narrative assignment on individual and personal explorations of racism

Source: Schaub, 2020.

Appendix 2

I have included several papers in this appendix. I think this appendix is interesting reading for people within Secwepemcúĺecw. It is here to make these documents more available, as sessional papers are complicated documents to search.

This appendix may inform us the Red Bridge is called Red because of wood colour or for perceptions by white settlers of skin colour. In my opinion, the popular notion that there were no "issues," racial or other, in the Kamloops area would not be verified by the reading of these components of the papers.

From "Papers relating to Indian Land Question. 1875."

Attorney-General Walkem to the Superintendent of Indian Affairs., Attorney-General's Office. 26th December, 1873.
SIR, – As I am aware that your attention has been drawn to the Cache Creek telegram, reported in the Dominion Herald, stating that the Indians has [*sic*] assumed a hostile attitude to the whites, I need not of course further refer to its substance.

I feel it my duty, however, to state that the matter is of a character too serious to be overlooked. From enquiries I have made, I find that one Mr. Ranald McDonald, who lives near Cache Creek, has informed Mr. Barnston by letter that the real cause of the discontent is the fact that you have paid them a visit, and that they feel they have been neglected by the Indian Department. Coming from such a source, I believe the information to be correct, and, under the circumstances, permit me to say that an immediate personal visit by you is due to the whites and as well as to the Indians, as the threatened danger may thus be easily averted, without expense or – the still more serious contingency – loss of life. I take the liberty of pressing the suggestion upon your attention at once, as the prevention by such simple means is far more desirable than any future remedy which may be devised to meet losses which it may be beyond human power to repair or redress. I have, &c. [signature] GEO. A. WALKEM.

The Superintendent of Indian Affairs to the Attorney-General. Indian Office, Victoria, 29th December, 1873.
SIR, – I have the honour to acknowledge your letter of the 26th instant, respecting threatened Indian troubles at Cache Creek, and calling my attention to a letter received by Mr. Barnston from one Ranald McDonald. In reply I have to state that it is my intention to proceed to New Westminster to-morrow morning (should I receive no telegram to the contrary during the day), and, if upon further enquiry, I find that the report has any reliable basis, my journey will be extended to Cache Creek at once. At the same time, you will permit me to doubt the correctness of the authority you quote, especially since there are so many gentlemen lately from the district in question, at present in this city, who can give more valued evidence. From all I can learn, the fear that they will lose their land and not be sufficiently provided for in this respect, is the real cause of disturbance if, indeed, there be any among the Indians.

May I beg to bring to your notice a letter addressed by me to the Honourable Provincial Secretary on Saturday, on the subject of these lands, and to solicit the action of the Government thereon, if possible, at once. Again I have to express the hope that no extensive leases of grazing lands in the vicinity of Indian habitations, will be given by the Government until their reserves are fixed, and, I assure you, the most fruitful source of anxiety or fear of injustice on their part will be avoided. I have, &c., [signature] I. W. POWELL.

The Superintendent of Indian Affairs to the Provincial Secretary. Indian Office, Victoria, 27th December, 1873.
Sir, – In view of a possible visit to Cache Creek and other Indians, among whom there are rumours which have reached me of threatened trouble, I have the honour to request that the quantity of land to be reserved for Indians east of the Cascades should be forty acres for each Indian family, instead of twenty, as agreed upon.

My reason for applying for the increased quantity is, that the interior Indians are nearly all possessed of horses and cattle, and I am convinced that twenty acres would not be found to be sufficient.

Should a personal inspection prove the correctness of my impression on this matter, it would be both highly important and practical in quieting all their fears of future injustice, if I could promise that an additional quantity of land would be laid aside for the grazing purposes of each tribe.

I might remind you that this principle is recognized in the present pre-emption law for white settlers, where 320 acres are allowed each individual east of the Cascades and 160 acres west of the same. I have, &c., [signature] I. W. POWELL

The Provincial Secretary to the Superintendent of Indian Affairs. Provincial Secretary's Office, 29th December, 1873.
Sir, – I have the honor to acquaint you with reference to your letter of the 27thinst., conveying a suggestion that the grant to a native family should be increased on the east side of the Cascade Range to from twenty to forty acres of land, that larges reserves of land have already been made in these districts.

The subject, however, will receive the mature consideration of the Government, meanwhile I have to request you will be good enough to confer with the Attorney-General on the subject. I have, etc., [signature] JOHN ASH.

The Attorney-General to the Superintendent of Indian Affairs. Attorney-General's Office, December 29th, 1873.
Sir – Your letter of the 27th inst., to the Honourable Provincial Secretary, on behalf of the Indians east of the Cascade Range, for tracts of forty instead of twenty acres of land as a bonus to each family, has been referred to me with instructions from the Committee in Council to confer with you upon the subject.

I called at your office and at your dwelling about 21/2 p.m. to-day, but was not fortunate enough to find you.

I have since received your letter of this date, informing me of your determination to proceed to-morrow by steamer to New Westminster, and thence to Cache Creek (should you receive no replies to your telegrams), to confer with the Indians of the interior. Permit me to say that I feel convinced that you have acted wisely in this serious mater. I would, however, suggest that no matter what peaceful assurances you may receive by telegraph, that it would be better to pay the Indians a visit than to stop short at New Westminster.

The Indians are certainly entitled to such a small piece of attention, accomplished too at such small expense, though it must be admitted that you cannot but encounter personal discomfort by reason of the inclemency of the weather.

As to the extra twenty acres asked for by you, as above stated, I have the honour to draw your attention to the list of, really in some instances, enormous, and in all cases, sufficient reserves, already laid aside for the Indians residing near Cache Creek, Kamloops, Okanagan, Shuswap, and other places. They cannot be, and as I have been credibly informed are not, dissatisfied with the amount of land allotted to them. On the contrary you will, after looking at your plans copied from the official records, agree with me that many of the reserves must by cut down, being out of all proportion to the strength of the tribes to which they have been respectively granted in days gone by, when land in the vicinity referred to seems to have been considered of little value.

When the reserves near Cache Creek, and some of the other places mentioned, were set apart, a conference was held with each of the Chiefs before any decision was arrived at. Their views were ascertained and their wishes were fully consulted. A parchment sketch of each reserve, enclosed in a tin case, was handed to them, and they expressed themselves entirely satisfied. The tribes now dread the idea of being placed upon and confined to these reserves, as they have ascertained that the Indian department intend, if possible, to carry out such a course.

The Indians speak freely upon the subject, and intimate their intention of resisting such a step. This is the cause of their dissatisfaction, and they wish to see you about it.

They are fully aware of your appointment and position, and to my personal knowledge they have expected a visit from you for nearly eight months back.

They, moreover, expect the usual presents from you as the representative of the great Chief, and in this I would respectfully suggest that you do not disappoint them. A few hundred dollars' worth of blankets, clothing, food, &c., would be well laid out if given to them.

I trust that you will excuse me for thus trespassing upon questions of an official character, of which you must necessarily possess a more intimate knowledge than I do. It is only a suggestion which I venture to make, as it might be overlooked in the hurry of an unexpected visit. I consider that whether the Indians are peaceably disposed or not that presents should be given, especially as the conference proposed by you is the first of its kind, and is one which they should always recollect with pleasure. I have, &c., [signature] GEO. A. WALKEM.

P.S. – Having seen you upon the subject of the foregoing, and as Mr. DeCosmos stated that there would be no difficulty in granting any extra lands to the Indians if absolutely necessary, and as your views and mine coincide as to a just treatment of the Indians, I take the responsibility of stating that you may tell the Indians that where the lands occupied by them are only suitable for grazing purposes and are inadequate to meet their wants, that twenty acres more than the twenty now conceded, should be given to each Indian family requiring them for pastoral use, regard, of course, being had in the disposition of the lands to the average acreage per family of all the reserves hitherto granted or hereafter added.

The Superintendent of Indian Affairs to the Attorney-General. Indian Office, Victoria, 12th January, 1874.

SIR, – I have the honour to inform you that owing to further telegrams which have been transmitted through the press, respecting the rumour of threatened Indian attacks upon the white settlers of the interior and your own wishes in regard to the same, I have determined upon proceeding at once to Cache Creek and Kamloops for the purpose of instituting personal inquiry into alleged grievances of the Natives, and if possible to allay for the present any hostile feeling existing on account of them. In addition to my own opinions upon this subject, as conveyed in my letter of the 27th ult., and which you were good enough to consider favourably for the purpose intended, I feel it my duty to report to you that among the assigned causes of discontent of the Indians, is the driving their cattle off unfenced lands or those held under pastoral lease. Once case has been reported to me of a judicial decision, in which an Indian was mulcted in comparatively large damages for alleged trespass upon lands which were not fenced, but held under a lease from the Government for pastoral purposes, a case which I am told has been taken up by many other Indians, and is said to form one of the prominent grievances for adjustment now. It would, perhaps, be invidious for me to reflect upon what certainly seems an injustice, but you will, I am sure, agree with me as to the necessity of ascertaining your opinion regarding the legality of such an issue, or in other words, whether cattle grazing upon unfenced lands, belonging to other than the holder thereof, can be subject to the penalty of trespass?

If these instances of grievance are correct, it is highly important in undertaking what may be a most grave and responsible mission, that I should be fortified by correct information upon all points likely to arise in the settlement of any complaint made by Indians. If, on the other hand, the leaseholder of an extensive tract of land is justified by law in driving Indian cattle off any unfenced portion and having the owner fined for damages, I fail at present to see how lasting disaffection is to be prevented, unless indeed, a far more liberal treatment is pursued toward them than the terms of Confederation would seem to justify on the part of the Dominion Government, or by the immediate passage or enactment of some local

Statute which would modify, if not change altogether, the existing pastoral land law which permits such apparent injustice. As I intend leaving early on Wednesday morning may I beg that you will be good enough to favour me with a replay some time to-morrow. I have, etc., [signature] I.W. POWELL

Telegram.

Clinton, January 9. – From Mr. Vasey, who lives on the Bonaparte, we learn that on Thursday last he was told by Father Grandidier, who was at Kamloops a few days previous, that, in a Council of Chiefs in that vicinity lately, seven were for war and two opposed. He (the Father) gave it as his opinion that the Indians were liable to commence hostilities at any moment.

A late decision of the Country Court, whereby an Indian was compelled to pay damages for trespass of his stock (the Indians claim, unjustly) has considerably agitated them. The leasing of large tracts of their grazing lands, and the non-arrival of the Indian Commissioner, as was promised them, add to their agitation. By these last reports, the excitement which prevailed among the settlers lately is again revived stronger than ever, and a general feeling of insecurity prevails. The Indians here who have been questioned regarding the matter deny all knowledge of it.

Appendix 3

TABLE A3. Perception Patterns: Basic Topic of Culture

Themes/Perceptions	Expression of Themes: Indigenous Participants				Expression of Themes: Non-Indigenous Participants		
	Educators	*Parents*	*Students*	*Community Members*	*Teachers*	*Principals*	*Senior Leadership*
Basic Topic of Culture							
Culture differences celebrated	0	1	0	0	5	9	1
Culture diversity identified	2	1	1	2	5	8	13
Culture used within colonial system	3	0	0	2	5	2	6
Culture understanding needed	10	5	3	9	0	6	8
Basic Topic of Community							
Connected to on community	4	0	0	3	1	6	4
Disconnected from own community	0	1	0	2	4	13	5
Lacking community	3	1	0	5	2	2	3
Building community	2	2	0	3	5	18	6
Existing community	1	0	0	0	4	3	1

	Basic Topic of Support						
Themes/Perceptions	Expression of Themes: Indigenous Participants				Expression of Themes: Non-Indigenous Participants		
	Educators	*Parents*	*Students*	*Community Members*	*Teachers*	*Principals*	*Senior Leadership*
Needed support recognized and met	0	0	0	0	9	4	1
Needed support recognized	8	1	1	9	21	12	15
Barriers to support	6	11	4	14	10	19	21
Support not available	9	3	0	10	0	0	5
Basic Topic of Attendance							
Attendance supports in place	0	0	0	0	0	1	0
Attendance supports needed	1	1	1	3	0	1	3
Poor attendance an obstacle to learning	2	3	1	3	1	9	9
Basic Topic of Trust							
Trust Existing	0	0	0	0	2	0	0
Trust restore/build	4	1	2	6	2	12	7
Trust lacking	8	4	3	12	10	18	18
Basic Topic of Statistics							
Stats perceived positive	0	0	0	1	0	5	4
Stats perceived negative	1	0	0	0	2	2	1
Stats assumed/needed	1	0	0	2	3	3	4
Basic Topic of Isolation							
Isolated by self	2	0	0	1	2	0	6
Isolated within the system	5	4	3	11	3	5	6
Isolated outside the system	1	1	2	2	0	7	4

Source: Schaub, 2020.

Education

Series Editors: Nicholas Ng-A-Fook and Carole Fleuret

Our *Education* series seeks to advance thought-provoking research within the broader field of education. Scholarly works in this series examine educational research from a multidisciplinary perspective and address a variety of issues in the field, including curriculum studies, arts-based education, educational philosophy, life writing, foundations in education, teacher education, evaluation, and counselling.

Previous titles in the *Education* series

Johanne Mainville, Sonia Di Lillo, Nathalie Poirier, and Nathalie Plante, *Creating Visual Schedules: The Schedule Evaluation Tool (SET) for People with Autism Spectrum Disorder and Intellectual Disabilities*, 2024.

Robert K. Crocker, *Religion and Schooling in Canada: The Long Road to Separation of Church and State*, 2022.

Timothy M. Sibbald and Victoria Handford, eds., *The Academic Sabbatical: A Voyage of Discovery*, 2022.

Joël Thibeault and Carole Fleuret, eds., *Didactique du français en contextes minoritaires : entre normes scolaires et plurilinguismes*, 2020.

Timothy M. Sibbald and Victoria Handford, eds., *Beyond the Academic Gateway: Looking Back on the Tenure-Track Journey*, 2020.

Anne M. Phelan, William F. Pinar, Nicholas Ng-A-Fook, and Ruth Kane, eds., *Reconceptualizing Teacher Education: A Canadian Contribution to a Global Challenge*, 2020.

Michelle Forrest and Linda Wheeldon, *Scripting Feminist Ethics in Teacher Education*, 2019.

William F. Pinar, *Moving Images of Eternity: George Grant's Critique of Time, Teaching, and Technology*, 2019.

Pierre Jean, *Planification de formations en santé : guide des bonnes pratiques*, 2019.

Thomas R. Klassen and John A. Dwyer, *Décrocher son diplôme (et l'emploi de ses rêves !) : comment maîtriser les compétences essentielles menant au succès à l'école, au travail et dans la vie*, 2018.

For a complete list of the University of Ottawa Press titles, please visit:
www.Press.uOttawa.ca

Milton Keynes UK
Ingram Content Group UK Ltd.
UKHW021251191124
451300UK00008B/283